Retirement, aka Unemployment for 25 to 30 Years!

Jeffrey A. Barnard | Barnard Financial Group

Jeffrey A. Barnard/Barnard Financial Group
1025 Old Roswell Road Ste. 104
Roswell, GA 30076

Book layout ©2018 Advisors Excel, LLC

Retirement, aka Unemployment for 25 to 30 Years! /Jeffrey A. Barnard. —1st ed.

ISBN 978-1717016133

Retirement is wonderful if you have two essentials:
much to live on and much to live for.

~ Unknown

Table of Contents

The Importance of Planning

Asking a financial professional about the importance of planning is like asking a fireman about the importance of water. The analogy has been stated in so many different ways: how can you hit the goal if you do not have one to shoot for; fail to plan and plan to fail; or to arrive at your destination, you need a roadmap, etc.

The Retirement Dilemma

Have you ever received a pink slip? Do you recall that feeling? A change in management, a corporate restructuring or just plain fired — losing a job or closing a business can bring the compounding effects of both financial and emotional panic. Depending upon your "station" in life and your ability to withstand weeks or months without income in the face of fixed expenses can be life changing.

Al loved his job; it was exciting and challenging every day. He loved providing a service to those he was responsible for, he loved the feeling of control as he handled and maneuvered the gigantic piece of equipment used in his line of work for more than 29 years, and the pleasure he enjoyed from his work was unlike many will ever experience. There was only one problem: He was a commercial pilot. For pilots, one day you are flying high above the clouds, soaring from city to city, and the next day, you turn age 65 and it's all over. He was done without a choice, rules of the sky.

Imagine being unemployed, by choice or not, for 25 to 30 years; that's retirement. It comes for us all. Some have the opportunity to choose when they want to retire, while others like Al have automatic retirement, or become disabled, or lose a job and, due to their age, can't get back into the workforce. Many of us, fortunately, will be able to pick a date and choose to close the door on the work phase of life, but no matter what the case, retirement brings life changes.

Life changes, but the expenses of life keep coming. The water bill will still come next month, the cable bill, groceries, property taxes, and the list goes on. Income will be needed next month, just like last month, but what level will your income need to be to replace the paycheck that was providing for your lifestyle? Plus, thanks to inflation, your expenses will increase over time, and you won't have the ability to control them. Planning to face those expenses on a fixed income can be a challenge, and it's a test that you cannot fail. The failure to plan for the inevitable period of your life when you can no longer work and need income to sustain you for 25 to 30 years, is a mistake, pure and simple.

Building the Estate

I am a confessed football nut. My infatuation started very young with a desire to play the game, but I did not live in an area where there were youth teams. Playing organized football for me began in 9th grade, when my mother finally gave in and let me play. It became a passion that lasted through my sophomore year at the University of Alabama, where I was fortunate to play two years for Coach Bear Bryant. This game taught me many life lessons I still use and live by daily. If you are around our office, you will frequently hear me using the game of football as an analogy in one way or another.

Preparation for the game of football requires hours of practice and personal sacrifice on behalf of the players, coaches and their families to achieve the goal of the team — to win. But to win, on game day, the execution must be sound. Preparation and execution is the core of financial planning, as well. Preparation not only can lead to success, but it can also help execute a plan that avoids unnecessary exposure to the risk factors that can unravel years of saving.

Preparation for retirement begins many years in advance of that day when you receive that proverbial gold watch. During what we call "the accumulation phase" of life, you are saving for the future. No matter what rule you use, whether it is the rule of saving 10 percent of your income each month, or saving in a 401(k) to get that company match, or accumulating alternative assets such as real estate to provide rental income, time is the most important component in the process. Using the advantage of compound interest coupled with the element of time can make this phase of life successful. Save for the rainy day, save all you can, because with the advancements in medicine, these days your retirement could last as long as 25 to 30 years.

Protecting the Estate

There is also a degree of planning you must do during the accumulation phase of life to stay on track and keep your estate moving down the road toward retirement.

Some of that planning may need to be purely defensive in nature to assure the completion of the first phase in your plan. Adequate life insurance can help make sure your plan completes itself for the benefit of those for whom you feel responsible, if you leave the game early. Liability insurance can provide a safety net for unforeseen accidents and situations that can derail your plan, and for that reason, we often recommend clients have an umbrella policy. Lastly, health insurance helps assure that you arrive without having a large slice of your retirement base spent on costs associated with staying healthy, to get there in the first place.

Along the way, there can also be pitfalls of the legal nature. A relationship with an estate planning attorney can provide the type of protection needed to help you get to the finish line. As I will explain in the estate chapter, documents like wills, trusts, and powers of attorney are essential in protecting the nest egg you are building.

Distributing the Estate

Retirement requires the transition from growing and accumulating assets to turning them into a sustainable and reliable stream of income. Preserving assets during years of retirement while facing various forms of risk, inflation, taxes, and out-of-pocket health care expenses creates challenges that require advanced planning.

For years, I have spoken in retirement seminars, taught workshops on various topics, taught classes on Social Security planning, addressed church groups and community functions. In every venue that I have spoken, I continually survey the audience with one simple question: "Do you have an income plan?" I am always astonished by the responses, or should I say, the lack of responses. While almost everyone saves and plans for retirement, very, very few have a plan for how they will take income from their accounts for the next 25 to 30 years. Add the different types of risk we must also consider, and the planning process now becomes more complex. I have chapters devoted to both taxes and health care, so let's take a look at how risk can play an important role in the retirement process.

Risk

In the financial arena, there are many different types of risk. Being unprepared to face all of the different types of risk can spell trouble for even those who have implemented a financial plan unless they are considered. A plan not only provides direction, but it should also be defensive as well. Unfortunately, those who enter the retirement years on a DIY-basis can be devastated by not defending against the ramifications these risks can carry.

Market risk is created when we invest in securities that will move up and down with the stock market. Interest rate risk is created by using fixed interest rates relative to a changing market, such as we might encounter when investing in CDs or long-term bonds, as both can be adversely affected by rising interest rates. There is longevity risk, which is the risk of having a long life and outliving your savings. Health care risk can come with the expenses of health care in aging due to out-of-pocket costs that may not be covered by insurance. As you can see, there are many forms of risk that can affect the value and purchasing power of your retirement savings, both during the accumulation and distribution periods of your life.

I want to address two additional areas of risk that I feel can have profound effects on the distribution phase if not considered in the planning process. These are inflation risk and sequence of return risk.

We all know about inflation. That bag of groceries you buy every two weeks will cost more each year. The effects of inflation reduce our buying power; in other words, our money just doesn't go as far as it once did. My first job out of college required that I move to Chattanooga. I was responsible for visiting insurance agencies in Alabama and Mississippi to explain the merits of using our company's product line. Due to the nature of my position, I would need a newer car for travel. The first car I purchased was a new 1980 Buick. It cost $ 8,200. Today, that same car, or a comparable car, would cost $ 30,000 or more. That's inflation.

Over the past 10 years, we have not felt the obvious effects of inflation in our daily lives because it has been suppressed. The Federal Reserve Board has artificially held down interest rates to aid in recovery from the Great Recession. However, this curtailing of interest rates has negatively affected fixed income savers, and these savers are some of the hardest hit by inflationary pressure. Retirees experience the effect of inflation as the constant chewing into their budget, requiring more and more dollars to buy food, staples, medications and keeping cars up to date.

A nugget that I try to share with every group I address is: "It's not what you have, it's what you spend". Obviously, you can reach a level of wealth that spending would never affect in your long-term plan. However, for most of us, spending, due to inflationary pressure over time, can place adverse pressure on our estates. How much you spend can have long-term effects on the longevity of your retirement assets.

Consider the hypothetical case of James and Brian. They are brothers and both have been quite successful. James is 67 and Brian is 65. They each have about $1.2

million saved for retirement. Both are married and have adult children who no longer live in the home. But there is a difference. James spends about $6,500 monthly with approximately 25 percent of that monthly expense going to charity and his home has no mortgage. Brian's family spends roughly $12,000 monthly to maintain their lifestyle. Using this hypothetical data, our planning software reveals that not only could James continue to follow his passion of supporting his charity, but that he and his wife would likely have sufficient retirement assets to endure a long-term care event and still leave a legacy for their children, even if they lived to age 100. Brian, on the other hand, may have a problem in the future. Unless changes are made in spending habits, he and his wife could exhaust their retirement savings by their mid to early 80s. It's not what you have; it's what you spend in retirement. See, Brian's $12,000 monthly living expense today is able to be maintained due to his current work income. But during retirement, due to inflation and the lack of work income, that monthly budget need may turn into $20,000 monthly and then eventually $25,000 monthly and, at that level, the estate will be systematically eaten alive. Remember, it's not what you have...

Sequence of return risk is a totally different animal of its own. This type of risk can have disastrous implications on retirement funds even before you reach retirement. First, what is sequence of return risk? This risk is created by the volatility of market returns. I have devoted a chapter to volatility later in this book, but for now let's address this particular type of risk. How you receive returns (positive or negative) and when you receive those returns on your investments, particularly while using them for income, can have an effect on their longevity over time. Negative returns early in the income phase can damage the longevity of your retirement assets. I have met and interviewed many who retired in 2001 and those who also retired in late 2007. In both cases, their retirement collided with a market slide that damaged the assets of almost everyone, as trillions of dollars of market value was lost. The greatest damage occurred to those who needed income from those depleted market positions. Many had to return to work, while others had to change their lifestyle to compensate for the change in income.

We know that securities are going to fluctuate in value, as their prices can be affected by more than just the profitability of the company. Many have witnessed world events, both natural and man-caused, change the value of their portfolios overnight. As we approach retirement, in that final two to three years before we flip the switch and transition from a growth investor to an income investor, we can ill afford a downturn in the value of our portfolio that must supplement our income. The first five years into retirement become very important. I want to segment my client's assets into those that will be needed to provide income with minimal or no exposure to market risk and those that can be exposed to market risk to provide a possible hedge against inflation over time. This, of course, depends upon the size of nest egg and the income needed to provide for retirement as well as other sources of income such as Social Security or a Pension. We want to move to a focus on yield; the real money of the investment world. In retirement, you must have yield.

Another football term we use to identify this two-to-three-year window of time is called the "Red Zone". In football, when a team reaches the 25-yard line of their opponent, they have entered the Red Zone. Here, the field has shortened relative to the goal line and play becomes more challenging. Entering the Red Zone during retirement requires that you begin to become conscious of the preservation of your principal. The necessity of using income from those assets can damage the assets' ability to re-grow if they have suffered a loss in value. For years, while you were working, when the market crashed, you could leave the monthly statements unopened and save yourself the stress of looking at the drop in value, because you did not need that asset for income. In most cases, the value of the accounts recover — eventually. But when you enter the Red Zone, we have a shortened time horizon, or period when we will need income from those assets to supplement our base income. The possible negative effect of that unpredictable sequence of returns must be managed, or your retirement nest egg can be damaged. Furthermore, you may not need additional income, but, as you age, you must take required minimum distributions (RMDs) from IRAs or 401(k)s beginning in the year following the year in which you turn 70 ½ . Unless you plan for this possibility, not only may you have to withdraw or sell positions that have lost value to meet the RMD, but it will also be taxable as income. Ouch!

Spending in Retirement

Another nugget I share with those we advise is: "It's not the first 10 years of retirement that matters, it's the second 10 years of retirement that really count". See, in the second 10 years, the effects of continually taking income from your assets can begin to manifest. I have often heard people state, if they knew how long they were going to live, they would know how much they could spend without running out of money. If it could only be that simple. Not knowing what expenses we will encounter, along with some of the heartache the future may bring, are two of the great unknowns. We can only prepare and plan to be ready.

The Bureau of Labor Statistics tells us that, during the first 10 years of retirement — often referred to as the "go-go" phase — your expenses are higher and you spend more discretionary money. During this period, there is fun, travel, possible hobby-jobs and volunteering. And did I say fun?[1]

For 33 years, Kurt arose at 4 a.m. to be at work by 6 a.m. Now in retirement, he told me he stays up some nights until after midnight reading or watching television. He said at first, he felt guilty in not following his routine of so many years, but he only felt guilty for a couple of weeks. All is good now. That's his version of go-go!

In the second 10 years of retirement, many retirees enter the "slow-go" phase. Expenses begin to drop as we begin to slow down. However, inflation has been creeping up for 10 years and the same pool of money has to be used to fund your daily expenses. In this period of time, health care expenses typically begin to rise as well. More importantly, unless you have guarded a portion of your assets from market risk, you may begin to see the effects of market volatility on your portfolio when you need to take income from your investments.

I call the last station of life the "no-go" phase. Here, we may encounter advanced medical expenses, especially for a couple, where one of the two has an elevated risk of needing care. This health care level usually requires hands-on or standby assistance and is not covered by Medicare. Long-term care expenses are paid out-of-pocket

---

[1] Ann C. Foster. Bureau of Labor Statistics. December 2015. "Consumer Expenditures Vary by Age." https://www.bls.gov/opub/btn/volume-4/consumer-expenditures-vary-by-age.htm.

or from an insurance policy that was purchased to provide benefits in an assisted living community, a nursing home or home health care. Furthermore, the loss of a life partner can also mean a change in income from Social Security or the loss of pension income.

While in the accumulation phase, you cannot spend every dollar you earn, or you will not be able to save for the future. In retirement, your goal is to keep your expenses such that you do not have to depend upon all of the investment returns on your assets to create your income, either.

Only 18 percent of workers surveyed by the Employee Benefit Research Institute in 2017 said they had a high level of confidence in their savings and ability to retire. That leaves 82 percent of the population with uncertainty about their financial situations. My thought has always been, how could you take the first dollar from your savings without knowing how much you can take over time (adjusted for inflation and taxes) without running out of money? This underlines the importance of planning. Later we will touch on what to look for in an advisor to assist you in making these and other planning decisions during that all-important transition period.[2]

Any investment plan will be exposed to risk. An income plan can add certainty, as it will account for risk. It will provide for both growth-focused positions as well as the preservation of assets, since the goal is to build a stream of income that you cannot outlive. While some assets will provide for income, other assets can be allocated for growth potential, without pressure, to provide income

---

[2] Lee Greenwald. Employee Benefit Research Institute. March 21, 2017. "The 2017 Retirement Confidence Survey." https://www.ebri.org/pdf/briefspdf/EBRI_IB_431_RCS.21Mar17.pdf.

many years in the future. Above all, it is a plan. You can move forward with direction and confidence. The plan must be re-evaluated periodically so that both you and the advisor can stay on track when working toward a successful retirement.

In that all important second half of the game, just like football, you must protect the ball (your retirement nest egg), adjust your strategy when you enter the Red Zone (recognize that change is approaching), and have a game plan for success (develop an income plan)!

CHAPTER ONE

Longevity

Y ou would think the prospect of the grave would loom more frightening as we age, yet many retirees list the fear of running out of money in their twilight years as their No. 1 biggest fear.[3] This fear is, unfortunately, justified, in part because of one big factor: We're living longer.

According to the U.S. Census, in 1950, the average life expectancy for a 65-year-old male was 78, and the average for females was 81. In 2010, it was closer to 84 and 86, respectively.[4]

The bottom line of many retirees' budget woes comes down to this: They just didn't plan to live as long. Now, when we are young and in our working years, that's not something we necessarily see as a bad thing; don't some people fantasize about living forever, or at least reaching the ripe old age of 100?

---

[3] Lea Hart. Journal of Accountancy. Oct. 6, 2016. "Americans' biggest retirement fear: Running out of money." http://www.journalofaccountancy.com/news/2016/oct/americans-fear-running-out-of-retirement-money-201615242.html. Accessed Feb. 15, 2017.

[4] Social Security Administration. 2011 Trustees Report. "Actuarial Publications: Cohort Life Expectancy." https://www.ssa.gov/oact/tr/2011/lr5a4.html. Accessed Aug. 16, 2017.

However, with a longer lifespan, as we near retirement, we have a few snags. One is that our resources are finite — we only have so much money to provide income — but our lifespans can be unpredictably long, perhaps longer than our resources allow. Also, longer lives don't seem to equate with healthier lives. The longer you live, the more you will need to spend in health care, even discounting long-term-care needs like nursing homes. To underscore this point, one study found healthy people spend more money over the course of retirement than the unhealthy. Case in point: A 65-year-old man with diabetes was estimated to need $88,000 for future medical expenses (again, these numbers are health-related only, not accounting for long-term care) versus a healthy 65-year-old man, who would need $144,000.[5]

Of course, part of this is that we don't necessarily get to have our cake and eat it, too; our collective increased longevity hasn't increased the healthy years of our lives. Typically, our life-extending care is most widely applicable to the part of our lives where we will need more care, period. Think of a pacemaker at 85, or radiation pills for cancer at 78.[6]

"Wow, Jeff," I can hear you say, "Way to start with the good news first."

I know, I've painted a fairly grim picture. But all I'm concerned about here is the cost. It's hard to put a dollar sign on life, but that is essentially what we're talking about when we're talking longevity. Currently, about 40 percent

---

[5] HealthView Services. 2016. "The Cost of Living Longer." http://www.hvsfinancial.com/the-cost-of-living-longer/. Accessed Feb. 24, 2017.

[6] Guia Marie Del Prado. Business Insider. Sept. 10, 2015. "People are living longer — but there's a catch." http://www.businessinsider.com/people-living-longer-but-not-healthier-2015-9. Accessed Feb. 24, 2017.

of people 45 and older underestimate their likely lifespan by five or more years. That's a lot of time unaccounted for.[7] Living longer isn't a bad thing, it's just expensive, and one key to a sound retirement strategy is preparing in advance for that expense.

Talking about this subject really hits close to home. My daddy suffered from dementia and Alzheimer's disease for more than 13 years while my mother developed Parkinson's' disease and Lewy body dementia. While my father required care attendance during the last two years of his life, my mother needed around-the-clock care for seven years. They had both watched their parents need this type care and had saved and planned for these expenses. Mom was able to pay for her own medical care to the tune of $ 6,500 a month. This did not include another $3,000 monthly for living expenses like food, utilities and other home expenses. All in all, she spent more than $ 100,000 yearly for seven years and was still able to pass a legacy to me and my sisters. Planning by design to be prepared for this possibility allowed them both to stay in their home, be with their family in the environment they wanted and live out their lives on their own terms

Living longer may be more expensive, but it can be so meaningful when you plan for what-ifs and just-in-cases.

Retiring Later

Planning for a long life in retirement partly comes down to when you retire. While many people end up retiring earlier than they anticipated due to injuries, layoffs, family

---

7 United States Government Accountability Office Report to the Special Committee on Aging, U.S. Senate. September 2016. "Social Security: Improvements to Claims Process Could Help People Make Better Informed Decisions about Retirement Benefits." http://www.gao.gov/assets/680/679747.pdf. Accessed Feb. 24, 2017.

crises and other unforeseen circumstances, continuing to work past age 60 and even 65 is still a viable option for others and can be an excellent way to help establish financial comfort in retirement.

There are many reasons for this. For one, you obviously still earn a paycheck and the benefits that go with it. Medical coverage and beefing up your retirement accounts with further savings can be pretty significant by themselves, but the advantage of continuing your income is also that it should keep you from dipping into your retirement funds, further allowing them the opportunity to grow.

Additionally, for many workers, their 8-to-5 is more than just clocking in and out. Having a sense of purpose can keep us active physically, mentally and socially. That kind of activity and level of engagement may also help stave off many of the health problems that plague retirees. Avoiding a sedentary life is one of the advantages of staying plugged into the workforce, if possible.

So many people I meet are excited about early retirement in their mid-to-late 50s. For many of them, it's not so much about traveling or just staying home, but creating a new life. We see people starting businesses, becoming consultants, completely changing careers — even on a part-time basis — to finally do what they always wanted to do. They have accumulated assets, and now feel they can move in a different direction. Their life is truly just beginning.

One of my clients really didn't want to retire; she just wanted to change the view of her classroom. As a teacher, for many years she had taught college-level courses. Today, she is still teaching, but remotely, via the internet and through online classes. All she needs is an internet connection and she is able to teach her class from a boat, from a different country, or from a poolside lounge. That is true freedom!

Health Care

Take a second to reflect on your health care plan. Although working up to or even past age 65 would allow you to avoid a coverage gap between your working years and Medicare, that may not be an option for you. Even if it is, when you retire, you will need to make some decisions about what kind of insurance coverage you may need to supplement your Medicare. Are there any medical needs you have that may require coverage in addition to Medicare? Did your parents or grandparents have any inherited medical conditions you might consider using a special savings plan to cover?

These are all questions that are important to review with your financial professional so you can be sure you have enough money put aside for health care.

Long-Term Care

Longevity means the need for long-term care is more statistically likely. If you intend to pass on a legacy, planning for long-term care is paramount, since three-fourths of us will need it,[8] yet this may be one of the biggest, most stressful pieces of longevity planning that I encounter in my work. For one thing, who wants to talk about the point in their lives when they may feel the most limited? Who wants to dwell on what will happen if they no longer can toilet, bathe, dress or feed themselves?

---

[8] LongTermCare.gov. 2017. "How Much Care Will You Need?" https://longtermcare.acl.gov/the-basics/how-much-care-will-you-need.html. Accessed Feb. 24, 2017.

I get it; this is a less-than-fun part of planning. But a little bit of preparation now can go a long way!

When it comes to your longevity, just like with your goals, one of the important things to do is sit and dream. It may not be the fun, road-trip-to-the-Grand-Canyon kind of dreaming, but spend time envisioning how you want your twilight years to look.

For instance, if it is important for you to live in your home for as long as possible, who will provide for the day-to-day fixes and to-dos of housework if you become ill? Will you set aside money for a service, or do you have relatives or friends near at hand whom you would comfortably allow to help you? Do you have a preference for in-home care over nursing homes or assisted living? This could be a good time to discuss the possibility of moving into a retirement community versus staying where you are, or whether it's worth moving to another state and leaving relatives behind.

These are all important factors to discuss with your spouse and children, as *now* is the best time to address questions and concerns. For instance, is aging in place more important to one spouse than the other? Are the friends or relatives who live nearby emotionally, physically and financially capable of helping you for a time if you have an illness?

Many families I meet with find these conversations very uncomfortable, particularly when children discuss nursing home care with their parents. A knee-jerk reaction for many is to promise that they will care for their aging parents. This is noble and well-intentioned, but there needs to be an element of realism here. Does "help" from an adult child mean they stop by and help you with laundry, cooking, home maintenance and bills? Or does it mean they move you into their spare room when you have hip surgery? Are they prepared to help you toilet and bathe if that becomes difficult for you to do on your own?

I don't mean to discourage families from caring for their own; this can be a profoundly admirable relationship when it works out. However, I've seen families put off planning for late-in-life care based on a tenuous promise that the adult children would care for their parents, only to watch as the support system crumbles. Sometimes this is because the assumed caregiver hasn't given serious thought to the preparation they would need, both in a formal sense and with regard to their personal physical, emotional and financial commitments. This is often also because we can't see the future: Alzheimer's and other maladies of old age can exact a heavy toll. When a loved one gets to the point that he or she is at risk of wandering away or needs help with two or more activities of daily living, it can be more than one person or one family can realistically handle.

If you know what you want, communicate with your family about both the best-case and worst-case scenarios. Then, hope for the best and plan for the worst.

Realistic Cost of Care

Wrapped up in your planning should be a consideration for the cost of long-term care. Although the majority of us will need some degree of long-term care — including the 30 percent of us who may need up to five years of facility care — 60 percent of us underestimate the costs of nursing home care! That included participants of one survey who were over 50 years old but underestimated nursing home costs in their community by 27 percent of the actual cost.[9]

---

9 Life Plans Inc. Jan. 6, 2017. "Who Buys Long-Term Care Insurance? Twenty-Five Years of Study of Buyers and Non-Buyers in 2015-2016." https://www.ahip.org/who-buys-long-term-care-insurance/. Accessed Feb. 23, 2017.

Another piece of planning for long-term-care costs is inflation. Inflation disproportionately affects seniors by an average of 5 percent, and that is mostly due to medical inflation. Long-term care is a big piece of the inflation-disparity pie, which is part of why many find their estimates of nursing home care widely miss the mark.[10]

While local costs vary from state to state, here's the national median for various forms of long-term care (plus projections that account for a 3 percent annual inflation, so you can see what I'm talking about):[11]

Long-Term Care Costs: Inflation				
	Home Health Care, Homemaker services	Adult Day Care	Assisted Living	Nursing Home (semi-private)
Annual 2017	$47,934	$18,200	$45,000	$85,775
Annual 2027	$64,419	$24,459	$60,476	$115,274
Annual 2037	$86,574	$32,871	$81,275	$154,919
Annual 2047	$116,348	$44,176	$109,227	$208,198

---

[10] Mark Miller. WealthManagement.com. April 23, 2015. "Inflationary Effects on Seniors." http://www.wealthmanagement.com/retirement-planning/inflationary-effects-seniors. Accessed Feb. 23, 2017.

[11] Genworth Financial. April 2017. "Genworth 2017 Cost of Care Survey." https://www.genworth.com/about-us/industry-expertise/cost-of-care.html. Accessed Feb. 23, 2018.

Fund Your Long-Term Care

One big "doing it wrong" that I see are those who haven't planned for long-term care because they assume the government will take care of everything. But that's a huge misconception. The government has two health insurance programs: Medicare and Medicaid. These can greatly assist you in your health care needs in retirement but usually don't provide enough coverage to cover all of your health care costs in retirement. My firm isn't a government outpost, so we don't get to make decisions when it comes to forming policy and specifics about either one of these programs. I'm going to give the overview of both, but if you want to get into the details of these programs, you can visit Medicare.gov and Medicaid.gov.

Medicare

Medicare covers those older than 65 and the disabled. Medicare's coverage of any nursing-home-related health issues is limited. It might cover your nursing home stay if it is not a "custodial" stay, and it isn't long term. For example, if you break a bone or suffer a stroke and stay in a nursing home for rehabilitative care and then return home, Medicare may cover you. But if you have developed dementia or are looking to move to a nursing facility because you can no longer bathe, dress, toilet, feed yourself, take care of your hygiene, etc., then Medicare is not going to pay for your nursing home costs.[12]

---

[12] Medicare.gov. February 2017. "What Part A covers." https://www.medicare.gov/what-medicare-covers/part-a/what-part-a-covers.html. Accessed Feb. 23, 2017.

Medicaid

Medicaid is a program that the states administer, so funding, protocol and limitations vary. Compared to Medicare, Medicaid more widely covers nursing home care, but it targets a different demographic than Medicare: those with low incomes.

If you have more assets than the Medicaid limit in your state and need nursing home care, you will need to use those assets to pay for your care. You will also have a list of additional state-approved ways to spend some of these assets over the Medicaid limit, such as pre-purchasing burial plots and funeral expenses, or paying off debts. After that, your remaining assets fund your nursing home stay until they are gone, at which point Medicaid will jump in.

Some people aren't stymied by this, thinking they will just pass on their financial assets early, gifting them to relatives, friends and causes so they can qualify for Medicaid when they need it. However, to prevent this exact scenario, Uncle Sam has implemented the look-back period. Currently, if you enroll in Medicaid, you are subject to having the government scrutinize the last five years of your finances for large gifts or expenses that may subject you to penalties, temporarily making you ineligible for Medicaid coverage.

So, if you're planning to preserve your money for future generations and retain control of your financial resources during your life, you'll probably want to prepare for the costs of longevity beyond a "government plan."

Self-Funding

One way to fund a longer life is the old-fashioned way, through self-funding. There are a variety of financial tools you can use, and they all have their pros and cons. If your assets are in low-interest accounts (savings, bonds, CDs), you risk letting inflation erode the value of your dollar. Or, if you are relying on the stock market, you have more growth potential, but you'll also want to consider the possible implications of market volatility; what if your assets take a hit? If you suffer a loss in your retirement portfolio in early or mid-retirement, you might have the option to "tighten your belt," so to speak, and cut back on discretionary spending to allow your portfolio the room to bounce back. But if you are retired and depend on income from a stock account that just hit a downward stride, what are you going to do?

HSAs

These days, you might also be able to self-fund through a health savings account, or HSA, if you have access to one through a high-deductible health plan (you will not qualify to save in an HSA after enrolling in Medicare). In an HSA, any growth of your tax-deductible contributions will be tax-free, and any distributions that are paid out for qualified health costs are also tax-free. That can be a tax trifecta. Long-term-care expenses count as health costs, so, if this is an option available to you, that is one way to use the tax advantages to self-fund your longevity. Bear in mind, if you are younger than 65, any money you use for nonqualified expenses will be subject to taxes and penalties, and, if you are older than 65, any HSA money you use for non-medical expenses is subject to income tax.

LTCI

One slightly more nuanced way to pay for longevity, specifically for long-term care, is long-term-care insurance, or LTCI. As car insurance protects your assets in case of a car accident, and home insurance protects your assets in case something happens to your house, long-term-care insurance aims to protect your assets in case you need long-term care in an at-home or nursing home situation.

As with other types of insurance, you will pay a monthly premium in exchange for an insurance company to pay for long-term care down the road. Typically, policies cover two to three years of care, which is adequate for an "average" situation: 70 percent of Americans will need about three years of long-term care of some kind. However, it's important to consider that you might not be "average" when you are preparing for long-term-care costs; 20 percent of today's 65-year-olds will need care for longer than five years.[13]

Now, there are a few oft-cited components of LTCI that make it unattractive for some:

- Expense — LTCI is expensive. It is generally less expensive the younger you are, but a 60-year-old couple who purchased LTCI in 2016 could expect to pay $2,010 each year for an average three-year coverage plan. And the annual cost only increases from there the older you are. That price was a 7 percent decrease from the year before, which seems promising, although the American Association for Long-Term Care Insurance credited that price decrease to the fact that several high-cost policy providers dropped out of the market, which leads to the next point. ...
- Limited options — Let's face it: LTCI is expensive for consumers, but it is also expensive for

[13] LongTermCare.gov. 2017. "How Much Care Will You Need?" https://longtermcare.acl.gov/the-basics/how-much-care-will-you-need.html. Accessed Feb. 24, 2017.

companies that offer it. With fewer companies willing to take on that expense, that narrows the market, meaning opportunities to price shop for plans with different options or custom plans are limited.

- If you know you need it, you can't get it — Insurance companies that offer LTCI are taking on a risk that you may need LTCI. That risk is the foundation of the product — you may or may not need it. If you know you will need it because you have a dementia diagnosis or another illness for which you will need long-term care, you will likely not qualify for LTCI coverage.

- Use it or lose it — If you have LTCI and are in the minority of Americans who die having never needed long-term care, all the money you paid into your LTCI plan is gone.

- Possibly fluctuating rates — Your rate is not locked in on LTCI. Companies maintain the ability to raise or lower your premium amounts. This means some seniors face an ultimatum: Keep funding a policy at what might be a less affordable rate OR lose coverage and let go of all the money they paid in thus far.

After that, you might be thinking, "How can people possibly be interested in LTCI?" But let me repeat myself — 70 percent of Americans will need long-term care. Those are pretty steady odds. And, although only 8 percent of Americans have purchased LTCI, keep in mind the costs of nursing home care. Can you afford $7,000 a month to put into nursing home care and still have enough left over to protect your legacy? This is a very real concern: One study says 72 percent of Americans are impoverished by the end of just one year in a nursing home.[14] So, not to sound like a broken record, but it is vitally important to have a plan in place to deal with longevity and long-term care if you intend to leave a financial legacy.

In every meeting with a prospective client, I ask, "How do you feel about planning for long-term care needs?" The answers I get vary from "I really haven't thought about it," to "That's why we are here, to learn about what we need to do," or "I have children who will take care of me."

I personally and professionally feel you need to address how you can realistically approach paying for care at some point. The care I am referencing is not hospital stays or doctor visits, but help with activities of daily living (ADLs). Things like bathing, dressing, meal preparation and medication management: all not covered by Medicare. These activities are private pay or paid by some form of long-term care insurance. It's all about having options and preserving assets.

In building a financial model, I explore the potential ramifications of this level of expense and its effect on an estate. For the individual, a spenddown of assets can be devastating, but not nearly as problematic as for the couple who will have a surviving spouse who must continue to live off the asset income that remains. Earlier, I shared my family's walk down the road of care need. What I didn't say is that if my mom had gotten sick first or lived longer, due to her level of care, her expenses of around-the-clock care would have exhausted their retirement savings. If you had that crystal ball and just knew how those final years were going to play out, you could plan perfectly for the future.

---

[14] A Place for Mom. April 30, 2015. "Long-Term Care Insurance: Costs & Benefits." http://www.aplaceformom.com/senior-care-resources/articles/long-term-care-costs. Accessed Feb. 24, 2017.

Today, there are many options to address what I call the care need issue. Planning with a financial advisor and addressing those different plans or how you will use your assets can give you peace of mind in facing these possible expenses in an environment of rising health care costs.

Product Riders

LTCI and self-funding are not the only ways to plan for the expenses of longevity. Some companies are getting creative with their products, particularly insurance companies. One way they are retooling to meet people's needs is through optional product riders on annuities and life insurance. Elsewhere in this book, I talk about annuity basics, and here's a brief overview: Annuities are insurance contracts. You pay the insurance company a premium, either as a lump sum or as a series of payments over a set amount of time, in exchange for guaranteed income payments. One of the advantages of an annuity is that it has access to riders, which allow you to tweak your contract for a fee, usually about 1 percent of the contract value annually. One annuity rider that some companies offer is a long-term-care rider. If you have an annuity with a long-term-care rider and are not in need of long-term care, your contract behaves as any annuity contract would — nothing changes. Generally speaking, if you reach a point when you can't perform multiple functions of daily life on your own, you notify the insurance company, and a representative will turn on those provisions of your contract.

Like LTCI, different companies and products offer different options. Some annuity long-term-care riders offer coverage of two years in a nursing home situation. Others cap expenses at two times the original annuity's value. It greatly depends. Some people prefer this option because there isn't a "use-it-or-lose-it" piece; if you die without ever having needed long-term care, you still will have had the income benefit from the base contract. Still, as with any annuities or insurance contracts, there are the usual restrictions and limitations. Withdrawing money from the contract will affect future income payments, early distributions can result in a penalty, income taxes may apply and, because the insurance company's solvency is what guarantees your payments, it's important to do your research about the insurance company you are considering purchasing a contract from.

Understandably, a discussion on long-term care and its particulars is bound to feel at least a little tedious. Yet, this is a critical piece of planning for income in retirement, particularly if you want to leave a legacy.

Over my four decades in the financial services industry, I have encountered many situations and have seen many things. Some repeat themselves, but even with that repetition, there are stories that still touch me and remain with me, years later.

Stephen and Gwen visited me in 2014. He was a tall man and Gwen was small and petite. She had Alzheimer's disease that was quite advanced. It was obvious from the way she was dressed that he had dressed her. They had no children and no other living family members. Stephen, who was in visibly poor health, had just had his third heart attack, during which he did not stay in a hospital. He went to the emergency room and then checked out — not even going to a doctor! — because they did not have a Medicare Supplement insurance plan, nor did they have any remaining assets. They only had the home they lived in. He was looking for an assisted living facility for Gwen, as he felt the next heart attack would take his life. The plan was to sell their home, which was dilapidated and run-down, and give those dollars to someone trustworthy to provide a place for her. Imagine, if you can, being in a place where, after 75 years of life, you have to make a choice to not accept the care you need because you cannot afford it.

Planning for retirement has many facets, and all must be considered to get both of you to the end of the line.

Spousal Planning

One thing to keep in mind no matter how you plan to save: Many of us will be planning for more than ourselves. Look back at all the stats on health events and the likelihood of long life and long-term care. If they hold true for a single individual, then the likelihood of having a costly health or long-term care event is even higher for a married couple. And you'll be planning for not just one life but two. So, when it comes to long-term-care insurance, or annuities, or self-funding, or whatever strategy you are looking at utilizing, be sure you are funding longevity for both of you.

I know I touched on this earlier in this chapter, but that hopefully can tell you how important this truly is. Aside from a long-term care event, just extending the income for a surviving spouse that may live an additional six to nine years past the first to die is not only frightening, but a stark realization I have come face to face with as I meet widows who are walking that path.

With the invariable change in income that will take place as one spouse dies and leaves only the larger of the two Social Security benefits for the survivor, the surviving spouse will need a new income model. Some of their expenses will be reduced, but many of their day-to-day costs — utilities, housing, etc. — will likely stay the same, so they'll have to pull more from their assets to cover the loss in Social Security, not to mention the likelihood of needing increasing income for medical expenses as they age. It is important as your retirement income plan is being created for you to consider three plans: one for while both of you are living, and then one for each spouse, should the other die first.

Any assets like pensions or annuities that provide guaranteed income can be invaluable as you enter this stage of life. They can provide a foundation of sustainable and reliable income. This type of income source should not change or go away.

Utilizing the aforementioned riders, I have been able to not only position assets to provide lifetime income like a pension, but also to include long-term care riders to stretch dollars and help preserve other buckets of money during a prolonged care expense.

CHAPTER TWO
Taxes

Where to begin with taxes? Perhaps by acknowledging we all bear responsibility for the resources we share. Roads, bridges, schools ... It is the patriotic duty of every American to pay their fair share of taxes. Many would agree with me, though, that while they don't mind paying their fair share, they're not interested in paying one cent more!

Now, just talking taxes probably takes your mind to April, tax season. You are probably thinking about all the forms you collect and how you file. Perhaps you are thinking about your certified public accountant or another qualified tax professional and saying to yourself, "I've already got taxes taken care of, thanks!"

However, what I see when people come into my office is that their relationship with their tax professional is purely a January through April relationship. That means they may have a tax professional, but not a tax *planner*.

What I mean by that is tax planning extends beyond filing taxes. In April, we are required to do an accounting with the IRS to make sure we have paid up on our bill or to settle the score if we have overpaid. But real tax planning is about making each financial move in a way that allows you to keep the most money in your pocket and out of Uncle Sam's.

Now, as a caveat, I want to emphasize that I am not a CPA, nor am I a tax planner, but I see the way taxes affect my clients, and I have plenty of experience helping clients with tax-efficient strategies in their retirement plans, in conjunction with their tax professionals.

I have developed a network of "go-to" professionals. These tax professionals are versed in different aspects of tax planning. My clients' needs range from simple tax preparation to those with Sub S Corporations, a charitable trust or maybe an irrevocable trust, each possibly requiring specialized knowledge.

It is especially important to me to help my clients develop tax-efficient strategies in their retirement plans because each dollar they can keep in their pockets is a dollar we can put to work.

Dillon and Monica in their mid-60's each had accumulated a sizeable IRA and had retired the year before I met them. They were meeting their expenses with just their Social Security income and were enjoying not paying any taxes. In our planning process, we taught them about the tax "time bomb" that was coming in the form of required minimum distributions at age 70 ½. Using an income strategy coupled with the relationship they had created with their CPA, they were able to proactively begin taking income from the IRAs and systematically convert funds to a Roth IRA to lower the higher forced income taxes they were facing in the future.

The Fed

Now, in the United States, taxes can be a rather uncertain proposition. Currently, with a Republican-controlled Congress and an Administration that places a hefty emphasis on protecting personal property rights, it would be easy to assume tax rates will decline in the next four to eight years. However, there is one (large!) factor that we, as a nation, must confront: the national debt.

Currently, according to NationalDebtClock.com, we are close to $20,000,000,000,000 in debt and climbing. That's $20 TRILLION with a T. With just $1 trillion, you could park it in the bank at a zero interest rate and still spend more than $54 million every day for 50 years without hitting a zero balance.

Even if Congress got a handle and stopped that debt from its daily compound, divided by each taxpayer, we each would owe about $167,000. So, will that be check or cash?

My point here isn't to give you anxiety. I'm just saying, even with the rosiest of outlooks on our personal income tax rates, you cannot count on low tax rates for the long term. Instead, you and your network of professionals (tax, legal and financial) should constantly be looking for ways to take advantage of tax-saving opportunities as they come. After all, the best "luck" is when proper planning meets opportunity.

So, how can we get started?

Know Your Limits

One of the foundational pieces of tax planning is knowing what tax bracket you are in based on your income after subtracting pre-tax or untaxed assets. Your income taxes are based on is everything on which you have to pay taxes.

One reason to know your income tax rate is so you can see how far away you are from the next lower or higher tax bracket. This is particularly important when it comes to decisions such as gifting and Roth IRA rollovers.

For instance, based on the 2017 tax table, Mallory and Ralph's taxable income was just over $240,000, putting them in the 33 percent tax bracket and $7,000 above the upper end of the 28 percent tax bracket. They already maxed out their retirement funds' tax-exempt contributions for the year. Their daughter, Gloria, was a sophomore in college. This couple shaved $2,300 off their tax bill by using that $7,000 to reduce their taxable income by helping Gloria out with groceries and school — something they were likely to do, anyway, but now deliberately put to work for them in their overall financial strategy.

Now, I use Mallory and Ralph only as an example — your circumstances may be different — but I think this nicely illustrates the way planning ahead for taxes can save you money.

Assuming a Lower Tax Rate

Many people anticipate being in a lower tax bracket in retirement. It makes sense: You won't be contributing to retirement funds, you'll be drawing from them. And you won't have all those work expenses — work clothes, transportation, etc.

Yet, do you really plan on changing your lifestyle after retirement? Do you plan to cut down on the number of times you eat out, scale back vacations and skimp on travel?

What I see in my office is that many couples spend more in the first few years, or maybe the first decade, of retirement. Sure, later on, that may taper off, but usually only just in time for their budget to be eaten up in health and long-term care expenses. Do you see where this is going? Many people plan as though their taxable income will be lower in retirement and are surprised when the tax bills come in and look more or less the same as they used to. It's better to plan for the worst and hope for the best, wouldn't you agree?

401(k)/IRA

One sometimes unexpected piece of tax planning in retirement is in your 401(k) or IRA. Most of us have one of these accounts or an equivalent. Throughout our working lives, we pay in, dutifully socking away a portion of our earnings in these tax-deferred accounts. There's the rub: tax-deferred. Not tax-free. Very rarely is anything free of taxation, when you get down to it. Using 401(k)s and IRAs in retirement is no different. The taxes the government deferred when you were in your working years are now coming due, and you will pay taxes on that income at whatever your current tax rate is.

Just to ensure Uncle Sam gets his due, the government also has a required minimum distribution, or RMD, rule. Beginning at age 70 ½, you are required to withdraw a certain minimum amount every year from your 401(k) or IRA, or you will face a 50 percent tax penalty on any RMD monies you should have withdrawn but didn't, and that's on top of income tax.

Of course, there is also the Roth account. You can think of the difference between a Roth and a traditional retirement account as the difference between taxing the seed and taxing the harvest. Because Roths pay taxes on the front end, there aren't tax penalties for early withdrawals of the principal, nor are there taxes on the growth after you reach age 59 ½. And, perhaps best of all, there are no RMDs. Of course, you must own a Roth account for a minimum of five years before you are able to take advantage of all of its features.

This is one more area where it pays to be aware of your tax bracket. Some people may find it advantageous to "convert" their traditional retirement account funds to Roth account funds in a year they are in a lower tax bracket. Others may opt to put any excess RMDs from their traditional retirement accounts into other products, like stocks or insurance.

Does that make your head spin? Understandable. That's why it's so important to work with a financial professional and tax planner who can help you not only execute these sorts of tax-efficient strategies but also help you understand what you are doing and why.

I urge all of my clients to visit their tax professional twice each year: once during tax season, but also a second time in the fall each year to take advantage of end-of-the-year planning. Good record-keeping habits and the ability to use tax software today can put you in the position to maximize the planning process later down the road.

One client of mine, Jennifer, was able to use deductions of her medical expenses and charitable giving to offset income by making that second visit to her tax professional. Being able to implement this change lowered her adjusted gross income to the point that she no longer paid income tax on her Social Security income.

A successful retirement requires being conscious and maintaining awareness about your goals and a changing landscape!

CHAPTER THREE

Market Volatility

U p and down. Roller coaster. Merry-go-round. Bulls and bears. Peak-to-trough.

Sound familiar? This is the language we use to talk about the stock market. With volatility and spikes, even our language is jarring, bracing, vivid.

Still, financial strategies tend to revolve around market-based products, for good reasons. For one thing, there is no other financial class that packs the same potential for growth, pound for pound, as stock-based products. Growth potential, outpacing inflation, new opportunities ... for these reasons, it may be unwise to avoid the market entirely.

However, along with the potential for growth is the potential for loss. Many of the people I see in my office come in still feeling a bit burned from the market drama of 2000 to 2010. That was a rough stretch, and many of us are once-bitten-twice-shy investors, right?

So how do we balance these factors? How do we try to satisfy both the need for safety and the need for growth?

For one thing, it is important to recognize the value of diversity. Now, I'm not just talking about the diversity of assets among different kinds of stocks, or even different kinds of stocks and bonds. That's only one kind of diversity, and it is important, but both stocks and bonds, while different, are still market-based products. Just as an incoming tide raises all boats, most market-based products tend to rise or lower as a whole, so diversity among stocks and bonds won't protect your assets during times when the market as a whole is in decline.

In addition to the sort of "horizontal diversity" you have by purchasing a variety of stocks and bonds from different companies, I encourage having "vertical diversity," or diversity among asset classes. This means having different product types, including both securities products and insurance products, with varying levels of growth potential, liquidity and protection, all in accordance with your unique situation, goals and needs.

Let's use the analogy of a football game to help look at this concept of vertical diversity among asset classes. With a football game, you have two halves of the game, both broken into quarters. If we breakup our approach to retirement planning in this way, we find we have an accumulation phase in the first half of our life and an income phase in the second half. We spend 35 to 45 years or longer putting together our nest egg during accumulation. As we approach retirement, we transition into a period where we begin to use those assets to provide needed income.

I like to use a simple guide called the Rule of 100 to help clients begin to identify how they will separate which funds are subject to market risk and which should hold more safely. Take 100 and subtract your age. Generally speaking, the number that represents your age should be held in relatively safer positions while the difference is held in various market risk positions. For example, a person who is 70 years old might consider holding 70 percent of their assets in relatively safer positions while holding 30 percent in various market-based risk positions. While the Rule of 100 is only a guide, it helps begin the process.

Once a ratio is established, I then proceed to a proper risk assessment to determine what level of risk is acceptable for whichever assets are in market positions. We may have reduced the total amount of money held at risk, but that amount could still be held either conservatively or aggressively in various market positions. My goal is to match the level of risk exposure a client is comfortable with accepting to the level of exposure in which the market assets are held.

The Color of Money

When you're looking at your overall portfolio diversity, part of the equation is knowing which products fit in what category: what has liquidity, what has protection and what has growth potential.

Before we dive into that, keep in mind that these aren't absolutes. You might think of liquidity, growth and protection as primary colors. While some products will look pretty much yellow, red or blue, others will have a mix of characteristics, making them more green, orange or purple.

Growth

I like to think of the growth category as red. It's powerful, it's somewhat volatile and it's also the category where we have the biggest opportunity for growth and loss. Sometimes products in the growth category have a good deal of liquidity but very little protection. These are our market-based products and strategies, so we're thinking mostly shades of red and orange. This is a good place to be when you're young — think fast cars and flashy leather jackets — but its allure often wanes as you get closer to retirement.

- Stocks
- Equities
- Exchange-traded funds
- Mutual funds
- Corporate bonds
- Real estate investment trusts
- Speculations
- Alternative investments

Liquidity

Yellow is my liquid category color. I typically recommend having at least enough yellow money to cover six months' to a year's worth of expenses in case of emergency. Yellow assets don't need a lot of growth potential; they just need to be readily available when we need them.

- Cash
- Money market accounts

Protection

The color of protection, to me, is blue. Tranquil, peaceful, sure, even if it lacks a certain amount of flash. This is the direction I like to see people move toward as they're nearing retirement. The red, flashy look of stock market returns and the risk of possible overnight losses is less attractive as we near retirement and look for more consistency and reliability. While this category doesn't come with a lot of liquidity, the products here are backed by an insurance company, a bank or a government entity.

- Certificates of deposit
- Government-based bonds
- Life insurance
- Annuities

401(k)s

I want to take a second to specifically address a product that many retirees will be using to build their retirement income: the 401(k) and other retirement accounts. Any of these retirement accounts, IRAs, 403(b)s, etc., are basically "tax wrappers." What do I mean by that? Well, depending on your plan provider, a 401(k) could include target-date funds, passively managed products, stocks, bonds, mutual funds or even variable, fixed and fixed index annuities, all collected in one place and governed by rules (aka the "tax wrapper") about how much money you can put inside and how you put it in, when you will pay taxes on it and when you can take it out. Inside the 401(k), each of the products inside the "tax wrapper" might have its own fees or commissions, in addition to the management fee you pay on the 401(k) itself.

Now, fees can be troublesome. You can't get something for nothing, and fees are how many financial companies and professionals make a living. Yet, it's important to recognize that even a fee of a single percentage point is money out of your pocket — money that represents not just the one-time fee of today but that also represents an opportunity cost. One study found that a single percentage fee could cost a millennial close to $600,000 in his or her lifetime.[15] For someone closer to retirement, how much do you think fees may have cost?

Even for those close to retirement, it's important to look at management fees and assess if you think you're getting what you pay for. Over the course of 10 years, those puppies can add up, and you may have decades ahead of you in which you will need to rely on your assets.

Dollar-Cost Averaging

With 401(k) et. al., when you are investing for the long term, dollar-cost averaging is a concept that works in your favor. When the market is trending up, if you are consistently paying in money, month over month, great; your investments are growing, and you are adding to your assets. When the market takes a dip, no problem; your dollars buy more shares at a lower price. At some point, the market will likely rebound, in which case your shares will fatten up and possibly be more valuable than they were before. This phenomenon is what we call dollar-cost averaging.

However, when you are in retirement, this may work against you. You may even hear of "reverse" dollar-cost averaging. Before, when the market lost ground, you were bargain-shopping; your dollars purchased more assets at a reduced price. When you are in retirement, you are no

---

[15] Dayana Yochim and Jonathan Todd. NerdWallet. "How a 1% Fee Could Cost Millennials $590,000 in Retirement Savings." https://www.nerdwallet.com/blog/investing/millennial-retirement-fees-one-percent-half-million-savings-impact/. Accessed March 14, 2017.

longer the purchaser; you are selling. So in a down market, you have to sell more assets to make the same amount of money as what you did in a positive market.

I've had lots of people step into my office to talk to me about this, emphasizing "my advisor says the market always bounces back and that I have to just hold on for the long term."

There's truth in that; thus far, the market has always rebounded to higher heights than before. But the prospect of potentially higher returns in five years may not be very helpful in retirement if you are relying on the income from those returns, for example, to pay this month's electric bill.

To combat having to either hold assets for a long period of time to rebound from a market correction or to avoid the potential pitfalls of reverse dollar-cost averaging, I use a strategy to segment assets based on their use and time periods.

Money that is needed for emergencies is held in a cash-like position of either checking, savings or money market accounts. It's ideal to earn interest or gains that might begin to offset inflation, but above all our aim here is having emergency funds be liquid.

Dollars we need to provide income should not be in positions that can be affected negatively in a market downturn. Because we need income from money held in this segment, we are seeking higher returns on more safely held positions. I like to utilize the fixed index annuity (FIA) in this segment for many reasons. The interest-crediting method in an FIA can provide for an opportunity to achieve higher returns than money held in cash-like positions, while not being exposed to downside market risk. With an optional rider, the FIA may provide for an enhanced lifetime income. But, most importantly, it will not lose value due to a market downturn.

My next segment is where we hold assets in an intermediate position. These dollars are designed to supplement money used from the emergency fund and to counter inflationary pressure. We'll want these assets to be available in nine to 12 years. Since the time horizon is relatively short, these must be held with that timeframe in mind. Positions that are affected by interest rate changes generally work well with this strategy.

Lastly, there's the long-term segment. These holdings will not be needed for many years, if ever. They also might be considered as a long-term health account. I feel the risk level on these holdings can be held at the higher level, as the time horizon is longer and they are allowed a recovery period, as it does not affect the income need.

However, it is important to emphasize the amount of money held in each position differs based upon the income needs of the individual or couple. The level of risk taken on any money during retirement must match a time horizon based upon the need for that money.

We all will experience the effects of inflation in our lives and we must prepare for its effects on our money, especially due to increasing longevity, since retirement may last for 25 years or more. That bag of groceries will usually cost more year after year. For that reason, we need market positions that, over time, can provide a hedge against the ravages of inflation.

I like to use yield positions from various holdings to both provide income on a reliable and sustainable basis while having assets set aside that, over the long-term, can manage exposure to volatility. Yes, the market will go up and down, as we have discussed, but dividends and yield income will hopefully give us consistent returns. We aim to position assets in a number of ways to hedge against inflation while also getting the income we'll need during retirement.

Is There a "Perfect" Product?

To bring us back around to the discussion of protection, growth and liquidity, the ideal product would be a "10" in all three categories, right? Completely guaranteed, doubling in size every few years, accessible whenever you want. Does such a product exist? Anyone who says yes is either ignorant or malevolent.

Instead of running in circles looking for that perfect product, the silver bullet, the unicorn of financial strategies, it's more important to circle back to the concept of a balanced, asset-diverse portfolio.

This is why your interests may be best served when you work with a trusted financial professional who knows what various financial products can do and how to use them in your personal retirement plan.

CHAPTER FOUR

Retirement Income

Retirement. For many of us, it's what we've saved for and dreamed of, pinning our hopes to a magical someday. Is that someday full of traveling? Is it filled with grandkids? Gardening? Maybe your fondest dream is just never having to work again, never having to clock in or be accountable to someone else.

Your ability to do these things all hinges on INCOME. Without the money to support these dreams, even a basic level of work-free lifestyle is unsustainable. That's why planning for your income in retirement is so crucially foundational. But where to begin?

It can be easy to be overwhelmed by this question. Some may feel the urge to amass a large lump sum and then try to put it all in one product — insurance, investments, liquid assets — to provide all the growth, liquidity and income they need. I think you need a more balanced approach. After all, retirement planning isn't magic. There is no single product that can be all things to all people, or even all things to one person, and no approach works unilaterally for everyone. That's why it's important to talk to a financial professional who can help you lay down the basics and take you step by step through the planning process. Not only will you have the assurance that you have addressed the areas you need to, but you will also have an ally who can help you break it down and help keep you from feeling overwhelmed.

Sources of Income

Thinking of all the pieces of your retirement expenses might be intimidating. But, like cleaning out a junk drawer or revisiting that garage remodel, once you have laid everything out, you can begin to push things into categories.

Once you have a good overall picture of where your expenses will lie, you can start stacking up the resources to cover them.

Social Security

Social Security is a guaranteed, inflation-protected federal insurance program that plays a big part in most of our retirement plans. From delaying until you've reached full retirement age or beyond to examining spousal benefits, as I discuss elsewhere in this book, there is plenty you can do to try to make the most of this monthly benefit. As with all of your retirement income sources, it's important to see how to make this resource stretch to give you the most bang and buck for your situation.

Pension

Another generally reliable source of retirement income for you might be a pension, if you are one of the lucky people who still have them.

If you don't have a pension, go ahead and skim on down to the next point, but if you do have a pension, let's take a second.

Because your pension can be such a central piece of your retirement income plan, you will want to put some thought into answering basic questions about it.

How well is your pension funded? Since the heyday of the pension, companies and governments neglecting to fund their pension obligations has been a persistent problem with this otherwise reliable asset. A 2016 report by CitiGroup revealed that there is a $376.6 billion shortfall between pension fund assets and pension obligations among the companies tracked by the S&P 500 index.[16] Is your pension one of those?

In addition to checking up on your pension's health, check into what your options are for taking your pension. If you have already retired and made those decisions, this may be a foregone conclusion. If not, though, it pays to know what you can expect and what decisions you can make, such as taking spousal options that will cover your husband or wife if he or she outlives you.

Also, some companies are incentivizing lump-sum payouts of pensions to reduce the companies' payment liabilities. If that's the case with your employer, talk to your financial professional to see if it might be prudent to do something like that or if it might be better to stick with lifetime payments or other options.

Your 401(k) and IRA

The "modern way" to save for retirement is in a 401(k) or IRA (or their nonprofit or governmental equivalents). These tax-advantaged accounts are, overall, a poor substitute for pensions, but one of the biggest disserves

---

[16] Matt Turner. Business Insider. Aug. 22, 2016. "Energy companies are facing another huge problem." http://www.businessinsider.com/energy-companies-are-facing-another-huge-problem-2016-8. Accessed Feb. 9, 2017.

we do to ourselves is to not take full advantage of them in the first place.[17]

Also, if you have changed jobs over the years, do the work of tracking down any benefits from your past employers. You might have an IRA here or a 401(k) there; keep track of those so you can pull them together and look at those assets when you're ready to look at establishing sources of retirement income.

Other Assets

- Do you have life insurance?
- Do you have any annuities?
- How about long-term-care insurance?
- Any passive income sources?
- Stock and bond portfolios?
- Liquid assets? What's in your bank account?
- Any alternative investments?
- How about rental properties?

It's important, if you are going through the work of sitting with a financial professional, to look at your retirement income picture, to pull together ALL of your assets, no matter how big or small. From the free insurance policy offered at your bank to the sizeable investment in your brother-in-law's modestly successful furniture store, you want to have a good idea of where your money is.

It's not uncommon to have one spouse paying the bills and managing the assets of a couple.

---

[17] Kelley Holland. CNBC Personal Finance. March 23, 2015.. "For millions, 401(k) plans have fallen short."
http://www.cnbc.com/2015/03/20/l-it-the-401k-is-a-failure.html. Accessed Feb. 8, 2017.

Scott and Jean fit this statement completely. While they are both involved in the income-producing side of their life, Jean runs the budget and sees to the management of their assets. They have three rental houses and have amassed a solid, diversified portfolio for retirement. When they visited with me, as Jean began to list their holdings, Scott was completely surprised at the total value of the estate. As we added it all up, Jean said, "I know how to do this, I know how to save, and I just let it grow in the 401(k)s, but I have absolutely no idea how to get income from this to live on. That's why we are here, we have built this, but now we need income from it."

Retirement Income Needs

How much income will you need in retirement? How do you determine that? A lot of people work toward a random number, thinking "If I can just have a million dollars, I'll be comfortable in retirement!" Don't get me wrong; it is possible to save up a lot of money and then retire in the hopes that you can keep your monthly expenses lower than some set estimation. But I think this carries a risk of running out of money. Instead, I work with my clients to find out what their current and projected income needs are and then work from there to see how we might cover any gaps between what they have and what they want.

Goals and Dreams

I like to start with your pie in the sky. A MassMutual study once found most of us spend more time planning our vacations than we spend planning our retirements.[18]

------

[18] Matthew Stern. BenefitsPro. Jan. 16, 2015. "Planning vacations more carefully than retirement."

Maybe it's because planning a vacation is less stressful: Having a week at the beach go awry is, well, a walk on the beach compared to running out of money in retirement. Whatever the case, perhaps it would be better if you think of your retirement as a vacation in and of itself — no clocking in, no boss, no overtime. If you felt unlimited by financial strain, what would you do?

Would an endless vacation for you mean Paris and Rome? Would it mean mentoring at children's clubs or serving at the local soup kitchen? Or maybe it would mean deepening your ties to those immediately around you — neighbors, friends and family. Maybe it would mean more time to do hobbies and activities you love. Have you been considering a second (or even third) act as a small business owner, turning a hobby or passion into a revenue source?

This is your time to daydream and answer the question: If you could do anything, what would you do?

After that, it's a matter of putting a dollar amount on it. What are the costs of round-the-world travel? One couple I know said their biggest priority in retirement was being able to take each of their grandchildren on a cross-country vacation every year. That's a pretty specific goal — and one that is reasonably easy to nail down a budget for.

Another goal aside from travel is the desire I see in many retirees to assist with the education of their grandchildren. Most are aware of the importance education played in their own successes. Some will fund a trust while many will contribute annually to a 529 college savings plan, and still others give what they can to help make it happen.

---

http://www.benefitspro.com/2015/01/16/planning-vacations-more-carefully-than-retirement. Accessed Jan. 12, 2017.

Current Budget

A current expense report is one of the trickiest pieces of retirement spending. Most people assume the expenses of their lives in retirement will be different, lower. After all, there will be no drive to work, no need to keep a formal wardrobe and, perhaps most impactful of all, no more saving for retirement!

Yet, we often underestimate our daily spending habits. That's why I typically ask my clients to bring in their bank statements for the past year — they are reflective of your ACTUAL spending, not just what you think you're spending.

A common question I ask during an initial interview is "Do you spend all of your income each month?" If you are spending all your net or take-home income, the transition to the fixed income of retirement can be difficult. I have to drill down to get to that real number.

I can't count the number of times I have sat with a couple, asked them about their spending, and had them give me a number that seems incredibly low. When I ask them about where it came from, they usually estimated based off of their total bills. Yet, our spending is so much more than our mortgage, utilities, cable, phone, car, grocery or credit card bills.

"What about clothes?" I ask, "Or dining out? What about gifts and coffees and last-minute birthday cards?" That's when the lights come on.

This is why I suggest collecting a year's worth of information. There is usually no such thing as a one-time purchase. Did you buy new furniture? Even if that is a rarity, do you think that will be the last time you EVER buy furniture?

Another big one is spending on the kids. Many of the couples I work with are quick to help their adult children, whether it's something like letting them live in the basement, paying for college, babysitting, paying an occasional bill or even just contributing to a grandchild's college fund. They aren't alone — 61 percent of Americans in 2015 said they had provided financial support for an adult child. And the more money you have, the more likely you are to have assisted your grown kids.[19]

My clients sometimes protest that what they do for their grown children can stop in retirement. They don't NEED to help. But I get it. Parents like to feel needed. And, while you never want to neglect saving for retirement in favor of taking on financial risks like your child's student debt, the parents who help their adult children do so in part because it helps them feel fulfilled. In the earlier-cited Pew study, more than 80 percent of parents said being able to help their grown children felt rewarding.

When it comes down to expenses, including and especially spending on your family, don't make your initial calculations based on what you COULD whittle your budget down to if you HAD to. Instead, start from where you are. Who wants to live off a bare-bones bank account in retirement?

Other Expenses

Once you have nailed down your current budget and your dreams or goals for retirement, there are a few other outstanding pieces to think about — some expenses that many people don't take the time to consider before making

---

[19] Pew Research Center. May 21, 2015. "Social & Demographic Trends: Family Support in Graying Societies—Helping Adult Children." http://www.pewsocialtrends.org/2015/05/21/5-helping-adult-children/. Accessed Feb. 9, 2017.

and executing a plan. But I'm assuming you want to get it right, so let's take a look.

Housing

Do you know where you want to live in retirement? This is a big piece of your income puzzle — since houses are typically the single largest asset owned by the middle class[20] — but one that often goes unaccounted for until the last minute.

Some people prefer to live right where they are for as long as they can. Others have been waiting for retirement to pull the trigger on an ambitious move. Whatever your plans and whatever your reasons, there are quite a few things to consider.

Mortgage

Do you still have a mortgage? What may have been a nice tax boon in your working years could turn into a financial burden in your retirement. After all, when you are on a limited income, a mortgage is just one more bill sapping your financial strength. It is something to put some thought into, whether you plan to age in place or are considering moving to your dream home, buying a house out of state or living in a retirement community.

Upkeep and Taxes

A house sans mortgage still requires annual taxes. While it's tempting to think of this as a once-a-year expense, when you have limited earning potential, your

---

[20] Patrice Lee. Independent Women's Forum. May 11, 2015. "Renting Widens the Wealth Gap?" http://www.iwf.org/blog/2797089/-Renting-Widens-the-Wealth-Gap-. Accessed Jan. 23, 2017.

annual tax bill might be something into which you put a little more forethought.

The costs of homeownership aren't just monetary. When you find yourself dealing with more house than you need, it can drain your time and energy. From keeping clutter at bay to keeping the lawn mower running, upkeep can be extensive and expensive. For some, that's a challenge they heartily accept and can comfortably take on. For others, the idea of yard work or cleaning an area larger than they need feels foolish.

For instance, Peggy discovered after her knee replacement that most of her house was inaccessible to her when she was laid up.

"It felt ridiculous to pay someone else to dust and vacuum a house I was only living in 40 percent of!"

Practicality and Adaptability

Erik and Magda are looking to retire within the next two decades. They just sold their old three-bedroom ranch-style house. Their twins are in high school, and the couple had wanted to "upgrade" for years. Now they live in a gorgeous 1940s three-story house with all the kitchen space they ever wanted, five sprawling bedrooms and a library and media room for themselves and their children. Within months of moving in, the couple realized that a house perfect for their active teens would no longer be perfect in five to 15 years.

"We are already paying the mortgage for this house, but we've started saving for the next one," said Magda, "Because who wants to be going up two flights of stairs to their bedroom when they're 78?"

Others I know have encountered a similar situation in their personal lives. After a health crisis, one couple found the luxurious tub for two they slaved over installing had

RETIREMENT, AKA UNEMPLOYMENT | 65

become a specter of a bad slip and safety risks. It's important to think through what your physical reality could be, whatever your long-term plan might be, and it's amazing how many people don't.

Contracts and Regulations

If you are looking into a cross-country move, be aware of new tax tables or local ordinances in the area you are looking to move. After all, you don't want to experience sticker-shock when you are looking at downsizing or reducing your bills in retirement.

Along the same lines, if you are moving into a retirement community, be sure to look at the fine print. What happens if you must move into a different situation for long-term care? Will you be penalized? Will you be responsible for replacing your slot in the community? What are all of the fees, and what do they cover?

Having worked with many people who have downsized from a home or condo to an assisted living community, I am no longer surprised when I hear a repetitive statement, "Why did I/we need all this stuff?" The transition to a single room or small apartment where care is readily available leaves little room for more than the important things, like pictures of family, some special mementos and necessary furniture.

Inflation

As I write this in late 2017, America has experienced a long stretch of low inflation, with inflation not exceeding 4 percent since 1991.[21]

---

[21] US Inflation Calculator. January 2017. "Historical Inflation Rates." http://www.usinflationcalculator.com/inflation/historical-inflation-rates/. Accessed Jan. 23, 2017.

However, inflation isn't a one-time bump; it has a cumulative effect. Even with relatively low inflation over the past few decades, the $20 sneakers you bought your grade-schooler in 1991 will cost $35.24 to buy for your grandchild.[22] What if, in retirement, we hit a stretch like in the late '70s and early '80s when annual inflation rates of 10 percent became the norm? It may be wise to consider some extra padding in your retirement income plan to account for any potential increase in inflation in the future.

Aging

Also in the expense category, think about longevity. We all hope to age gracefully. However, it's important to face the prospect of aging with a sense of realism.

The elephant in the room for many families is long-term care: no one wants to admit they will likely need it, but the reality is that 70 percent of us will.[23] Aging is a significant piece of retirement income planning because you'll want to figure out how to set aside money for your care, either at home or away from it. The more comfortable you get with discussing your wishes and plans with your loved ones, the easier planning for the financial side of it can be.

I discuss health care and potential long-term care costs in more detail elsewhere in this book, but suffice it to say that nursing home care is incredibly expensive and typically isn't something you get to choose when you need.

It isn't just the costs of long-term care that pose a concern in living longer. It's also about covering the possible costs of everything else associated with living longer. For instance, if Henry retires from his job as a

---

[22] Ibid.

[23] LongTermCare.gov. 2017. "The Basics." http://longtermcare.gov/the-basics/. Accessed Jan. 23, 2017.

biochemical engineer at age 65, perhaps he planned to have a very decent income for 20 years, until age 85. But what if he lives until he's 95? That's a whole third more — 10 years — of personal income he will need.

Putting It All Together

Whew! So you have pulled together what you have, and you have a pretty good idea of where you want to be. Now your financial professional and you can go about the work of arranging what you have to cover what you need — and how you might try to cover any gaps you have.

Like the proverbial man in the Bible who built his house on a rock, I like to help my clients figure out how to cover their day-to-day living expenses — their needs — with insurance and other guaranteed income sources like pensions and Social Security.

To do this, I use comprehensive planning software and years of experience to evaluate their income potential from the combination of guaranteed sources, asset income ability, inflation and taxes, also factoring in an estimate of long-term care expenses that may have to be paid from savings.

One of the most important elements in the retirement planning process is your expenses. Remember: It's not how much money you have in retirement; it's how much you spend. I analyze the accounts of people with more than a million dollars who will run out of money in their early 80s, while seeing others with a fifth of that amount of money who should have a legacy to pass to their children. Why? Because of what they spend. Take a monthly budget of $4,000, and in 20 years that income need can almost double.

I want to create an income plan that can help give clients the income they want or, more importantly, the income they need, which, through the combination of both investment and insurance products, may provide the path to a successful retirement.

Again, you should keep in mind that there isn't one single financial vehicle, asset or source that can fill all of your needs, and that's OK. One of the challenges of making a plan for your income in retirement is about figuring out what products to use. You can let go of some of that stress when you accept that you will need a diverse portfolio, with bonds, stocks, insurance and other income sources, not just one massive money pile.

One way to help shore up your income gaps is by working with your financial professional and a qualified tax advisor to mitigate your tax exposure. If you have a 401(k) or IRA, a financial advisor in your corner can help you figure out how and when to take distributions from your account in a way that doesn't put you into a higher tax bracket. Or you might learn how to use tax-advantaged bonds more effectively. Effective tax planning isn't about "adding" to your income; especially with retirement, it's less about what you make as it is about what you keep. Paying a lower tax bill keeps more money in your pocket, which is where you want it when it comes to retirement income.

Now you can look at ways to cover your remaining retirement goals. Are there products like long-term-care insurance that are specific to a certain kind of expense you anticipate? Is there a particular asset you want to use for your "play" money — that money for trips and gifting for the grandkids? Is there any way you can portion off money for those charitable legacy plans?

Once you have analyzed your income wants and needs and your realistic assets to cover them, you may have a gap. The masterstroke of a competent financial professional will be to help you figure out how you will cover that gap. Will you perhaps need to cut out a round of golf a week? Maybe skip the new car? Or will you need to take more significant action?

One way to cover an income gap is to consider working longer before retirement or part time even after that magical calendar date. This may not be the best "plan" for you; disabilities, work demands and physical or emotional limitations can stymie the best-laid plans to continue working. However, if it is physically possible for you, this is one big way to help your assets last, for more than one reason.

In fact, Americans are now setting the record in the developed world for working past age 65. While some workers do list their finances as a reason for doing so, many others cite feeling important, staying active, maintaining their health and having a sense of purpose as other reasons to stick with their jobs, even if only on a part-time basis.[24]

One woman, Natalie, 69, came into my office and bluntly started our visit with "I want to know if I can retire." I went through the process of modeling her financial situation and gathering information about her goals, etc. Midway through, she again asked, "Can I retire?" As I walked her through everything, it became clear that, though she had diligently saved and likely had more than sufficient assets to cover her anticipated expenses, she had lacked the comfort of having a comprehensive plan.

---

[24] Ben Steverman. Bloomberg. May 13, 2016. " 'I'll Never Retire': Americans Break Record for Working Past 65." https://www.bloomberg.com/news/articles/2016-05-13/-i-ll-never-retire-americans-break-record-for-working-past-65. Accessed Feb. 24, 2017.

Her whole demeanor changed after we worked with her to create — for the first time — a written plan designed to help her achieve the financial freedom she desired for retirement.

When you're retired, you no longer have an employer paying you a steady check. It is up to you to make sure you have saved and planned for the income you need.

CHAPTER FIVE

Social Security

S ocial Security is often the foundation piece of retirement income. Backed by the strength of the U.S. Treasury, it provides perhaps the most dependable paycheck you will have in retirement.

From the time you collect your first paycheck from whatever job made you a bonafide taxpayer (for me, it was 1980, when I became a Field Agency Manager for South Central Underwriters in Chattanooga, Tennessee), you are paying into the grand old Social Security system. What grew and developed out of the pressures of the Great Depression has become one of the most popular government programs in the country, and if you pay in the equivalent of 10 years or more, you, too, can benefit from the Social Security program.

Now, before we get into the nitty-gritty of Social Security, I'd like to address a current concern: Will Social Security still be there for you when you reach retirement age?

The Future of Social Security

This question is ever-present as headlines trumpet an underfunded Social Security program, alongside the flux of baby boomers who are retiring in droves, and the comparatively smaller younger generations who are bearing the responsibility of funding the system.

The Social Security Administration itself is a source of this concern as each Social Security statement now bears an asterisk that continues near the end of the summary:

> " *Your estimated benefits are based on current law. Congress has made changes to the law in the past and can do so at any time. The law governing benefit amounts may change because, by 2034, the payroll taxes collected will be enough to pay only about 79 percent of scheduled benefits."*

Just a reminder, as if you needed one, that nothing in life is guaranteed.

Before you get too discouraged, though, here are a few thoughts to keep you going:

- Although those who retire after 2034 may only receive 79 cents on the dollar for their scheduled benefits, 79% is notably not zero.
- Social Security has made changes in the distant and near past to protect the fund's solvency, including increasing retirement ages and striking certain filing strategies.
- There are many changes that Congress could make and that lawmakers are currently discussing to fix the system, such as further increasing full retirement age and eligibility.
- One thing that no one is seriously discussing? Reneging on current obligations to retirees or the soon-to-retire.

Take heart. The real answer to the question, "Will Social Security be there for me?" is still yes.

This question is an important one to consider when you take a look at how much we, as a nation, rely on this program. Did you know Social Security benefits compose an average of 34 percent of retired Americans' income? Nearly half of couples and more than 70 percent of unmarried people report their benefits make up more than 50 percent of their income.[25]

If you ask me, that's a pretty significant piece of your retirement income puzzle.

Another caveat? You may not realize this, but no one can legally "advise" you about your Social Security benefits.

"But, Jeff," you may be thinking, "Isn't that part of what you do? And what about that nice gentleman at the Social Security Administration office I spoke with on the phone?"

Don't get me wrong. Social Security Administration employees know their stuff. They are trained to know policies and programs, and they are usually pretty quick to tell you what you can and cannot do. But the government specifically says that, because Social Security is a benefit that you alone have paid into and earned, your Social Security decisions, too, are yours alone.

When it comes to financial professionals, we can't push you in any directions, either, BUT — there's a big but, here — working with a well-informed financial professional is still incredibly handy when it comes to your Social Security decisions. Why? Because someone who's worth his or her salt will know what withdrawal strategies might pertain to your specific situation and will ask questions that can help

---

25 Social Security Administration. 2016. "Fact Sheet: Social Security." https://www.ssa.gov/news/press/factsheets/basicfact-alt.pdf. Accessed Jan. 4, 2017.

you determine what you are looking for when it comes to your Social Security.

For instance, some people want the highest possible monthly benefit. Others want to start their benefits early, and not always because of financial need. I heard of one man who called in to start his Social Security payments the day he qualified, just because he liked to think of it as the government paying back a debt it owed him and enjoyed the feeling of receiving a check from Uncle Sam.

Whatever your reasons, questions or feelings regarding Social Security, the decision is yours alone, but working with a financial professional can help you put your options in perspective by showing you — both with industry knowledge and with proprietary software or planning processes — where your benefits fit into your overall strategy for retirement income.

One reason the federal government doesn't allow for "advice" related to Social Security, I suspect, is so no one can profit from giving you advice related to your Social Security benefit — or from providing any clarifications. Again, this is a sign of a good financial professional. Those who are passionate about their work will be knowledgeable about what benefit strategies might be to your advantage and will happily share those possible options with you.

Full Retirement Age

When it comes to Social Security, it seems like many people only think so far as "yes." They don't take the time to understand the various options available. Instead, because it is common knowledge you can begin your benefits at age 62, that's what many of us do. While more people are opting to delay taking benefits, age 62 is still firmly the most popular age to start.[26]

What many people fail to understand is that, by starting benefits early, they may be leaving a lot of money on the table. You see, the Social Security Administration bases your monthly benefit on two factors: your earnings history and your full retirement age (FRA).

From your earnings history, they pull the 35 years you made the most money and use a mathematical indexing formula to figure out a monthly average from those years. If you paid into the system for less than 35 years, then every year you didn't pay in will be counted as a zero.

Once they have calculated what your monthly earning would be at FRA, the government then calculates what to put on your check based on how close you are to FRA. FRA was originally set at 65, but, as the population aged and lifespans lengthened, the government shifted FRA later and later based on an individual's year of birth. Check out the following chart to see when you will reach FRA.

---

[26] Emily Brandon. Money, US News. "The Most Popular Ages to Sign Up for Social Security." http://money.usnews.com/money/retirement/articles/2015/06/01/the-most-popular-ages-to-sign-up-for-social-security. Accessed Jan. 5 2017.

Age to Receive Full Social Security Benefits*	
(Called "full retirement age" or "normal retirement age.")	
Year of Birth*	FRA
1937 or earlier	65
1938	65 and 2 months
1939	65 and 4 months
1940	65 and 6 months
1941	65 and 8 months
1942	65 and 10 months
1943-1954	66
1955	66 and 2 months
1956	66 and 4 months
1957	66 and 6 months
1958	66 and 8 months
1959	66 and 10 months
1960 and later	67

If you were born on Jan. 1 of any year, you should refer to the previous year. (If you were born on the 1st of the month, we figure your benefit (and your full retirement age) as if your birthday was in the previous month.)

When you attain FRA, you are eligible to receive 100 percent of whatever the Social Security Administration says is your full monthly benefit. This is why 66 is the second-most popular age to claim: Baby boomers largely reach FRA at 66.[27]

Starting at age 62, for every year before FRA you claim benefits, your monthly check is reduced by 5 percent. Conversely, for every year you delay taking benefits past FRA, your monthly benefit increases by 8 percent (until age 70 — after that, there is no monetary advantage to delaying Social Security benefits). While your circumstances and needs may vary, this is why a lot of financial professionals urge people to at least consider delaying until 70.

Why Wait?

Taking benefits early could affect your monthly check by _____.								
62	63	64	65	FRA 66	67	68	69	70
-20%	-15%	-10%	-5%	0	+8%	+16%	+24%	+32%

My Social Security

As long as you are over age 30, you have probably received a notice from the Social Security Administration telling you to activate something called My Social Security. This is a handy way to learn more about whatever your particular benefit options are and to keep track of what your earnings record looks like and the benefits you have accrued over the years.

---

27 Ibid.

Essentially, My Social Security is an online account that you can activate to see what your personal Social Security picture looks like, which you can do at www.ssa.gov/myaccount. This can be extremely helpful when it comes to planning for income in retirement and figuring up the difference between your anticipated income versus anticipated expenses.

One other way My Social Security is helpful? It's a great way to see if there is a problem. For instance, I have heard of one woman who, through diligently checking her tax records against her Social Security profile, discovered her Social Security check was shortchanging her, based on her earnings history. After taking the discrepancy to the Social Security Administration, they sent her what they owed her in makeup benefits.

COLA

Social Security is a largely guaranteed piece of the retirement puzzle: If you get a statement that says to expect $1,000 a month, you can pretty surely know you will get $1,000 a month. But there is one detail that is variable, and that is something called the cost-of-living adjustment, or COLA.

The COLA is an increase in your monthly check that is meant to address inflation in everyday life. After all, your expenses will likely continue to experience inflation in retirement, but you will no longer have the opportunity for raises, bonuses or promotions that you had when you were working. Instead, Social Security receives an annual cost-of-living increase tied to the Department of Labor's Consumer Price Index for Urban Wage Earners and Clerical Workers, or CPI-W. If the CPI-W measurement shows inflation rose a certain amount for regular goods and services, then Social Security recipients will see that reflected in their COLA.

The COLA averages 4 percent, but in a no- or low-inflation environment, such as in 2010, 2011 and 2016, Social Security recipients will not get an adjustment. Some see the COLA as a perk, bump or bonus, but in reality it works more like this: Your mom sends you to the store with $2.50 for a gallon of milk. Milk costs exactly $2.50. The next week, you go back with that same amount, but it is now $2.52 for a gallon, so you go back to Mom, and she gives you 2 cents. You aren't bringing home more milk — it just costs more money.

So the COLA is less about "making" more money and more about keeping seniors' purchasing power from eroding when inflation is a big factor, such as in 1975, when it was 8 percent![28] Still, don't let that detract from your enthusiasm about COLAs; after all, what if Mom's solution was "Here's the same $2.50; try to find pennies from somewhere else to get that milk!"?

Spousal Benefits

We've talked about FRA, but another big Social Security decision is about spousal benefits.

If you or your spouse has a long stretch of zeros in your earnings history — perhaps if one of you stayed home for years, caring for children or sick relatives — you may want to consider filing for spousal benefits instead of filing on your own earnings history. A spousal benefit can be up to 50 percent of the primary wage earner's benefit at full retirement age.

---

[28] Social Security Administration. 2017. "Cost-Of-Living Adjustment (COLA)." https://www.ssa.gov/cola/. Accessed Jan. 9, 2017.

To begin drawing a spousal benefit, you must be at least 62 years old, and the primary wage earner must have already filed for his or her benefit. While there are penalties for taking spousal benefits early (you could lose up to 67.5 percent of your check for filing at age 62), you cannot earn credits for delaying.[29]

Like I said, the spousal benefit can be a big deal for those who don't have a very long pay history, but it's important to weigh your own earned benefits against the option of withdrawing based on a fraction of your spouse's benefits.

To look at how this could play out, let's use a hypothetical example of Mary Jane, who is 60, and Peter, who is 62.

Let's say that Peter's benefit at FRA, in his case 66, would be $1,600. If Peter begins his benefits right now, four years before FRA, his monthly check will be $1,200. If Mary Jane begins taking spousal benefits in two years at the earliest date possible, her monthly benefits will be reduced by 67.5 percent, to $520 per month (remember, at FRA, the most she can qualify for is half of Peter's FRA benefit).

What if Peter and Mary Jane both wait until FRA? At 66, Peter begins taking his full benefit of $1,600 a month. Two years later, when she reaches age 66, Mary Jane will qualify for $800 a month. By waiting until FRA, the couple's monthly benefit goes from $1,720 to $2,400.

What if Peter delays until 70 to get his maximum possible benefit? For each year past FRA that he delays, his monthly benefits increase by 8 percent. This means that,

[29] Social Security Administration. 2017. "Retirement Planner: Benefits for You As A Spouse."
https://www.ssa.gov/planners/retire/applying6.html. Accessed Jan. 11, 2017.

at 70, he could file for a monthly benefit of $2,112. However, delayed retirement credits do not affect spousal benefits, so as soon as Peter files at 70, Mary Jane would also file (at age 68) for her maximum benefit of $800, so their highest possible combined monthly check is $2,912.[30]

When it comes to your Social Security benefits, you obviously will want to consider if a monthly check based on a fraction of your spouse's earnings will be comparable to or larger than your own earnings history.

I've thrown a lot of numbers at you to consider, like your FRA based on your year of birth, as well as a COLA and spousal benefits (and we haven't even gotten to taxes!), but here's another date to think about: Jan. 2, 1954. What's important about that, you ask? For those born on or after that date, you can only make the choice to withdraw your benefits one way, one time. That means you will have to pick whether to take a spousal benefit or use your own earnings history, and whichever one you choose will be the check you get every month for the duration of your retirement. However, if you were born BEFORE Jan. 2, 1954, read on.

If you were born before Jan. 2, 1954, you are eligible to change your benefit withdrawal strategy *even after you have begun withdrawals*. This means that you could begin taking a spousal benefit at 62 or FRA while allowing the benefits based on your own earnings history to accrue.[31]

---

[30] Office of the Chief Actuary. Social Security Administration. 2017. "Social Security Benefits: Benefits for Spouses." https://www.ssa.gov/OACT/quickcalc/spouse.html#calculator. Accessed Jan. 11, 2017.

[31] Social Security Administration. 2017. "Retirement Planner: Benefits for You As A Spouse." https://www.ssa.gov/planners/retire/applying6.html. Accessed Jan. 11, 2017.

Let's look back to Mary Jane and Peter to see how this could theoretically work. We know that if they both file at FRA, Mary Jane will receive $800 a month on top of Peter's $1,600 benefit when she files. But what if her own earned credit at FRA was $700? In four years, when Mary Jane turns 70, the monthly benefit based on her personal earnings will have grown from $700 to $924. At 70, she could file to trade up her $800 monthly spousal benefit for a $924 monthly check. Remember, this only works for Mary Jane if she was born before Jan. 2, 1954.

Divorced Spouses

There are a few considerations for those of us who have gone through a divorce. If you 1) were married for 10 years or more *and* 2) have since been divorced for at least two years *and* 3) are unmarried *and* 4) your ex-spouse qualifies to begin Social Security, you qualify for a spousal benefit based on your ex-husband or ex-wife's earnings history at FRA. A divorced spousal benefit is different from the married spousal benefit in one way: You don't have to wait for your ex-spouse to file before you can file yourself.[32]

For instance, Charles and Moira were married for 15 years before their divorce, when he was 36 and she was 40. Moira has been remarried for 20 years, and, although Charles briefly remarried, his second marriage ended after a few years. Charles' benefits are largely calculated based on his many years of volunteering in schools, meaning his personal monthly benefit is close to zero.

---

[32] Social Security Administration. 2017. "Retirement Planner: If You Are Divorced."
https://www.ssa.gov/planners/retire/divspouse.html. Accessed Jan. 11, 2017.

Although Moira has deferred her retirement, opting to delay benefits until she is 70, Charles can begin taking benefits calculated off of Moira's work history at FRA as early as 62. However, he will also have the option of waiting until FRA to collect the maximum, or 50 percent of Moira's earned monthly benefit at her FRA.

Widowed Spouses

If your marriage ended with the death of your spouse, you might claim a benefit for your spouse's earned income as his or her widow/widower, called a survivor's benefit. Unlike a spousal benefit or divorced benefits, if your husband or wife dies, you are allowed to claim his or her full benefit. Also unlike spousal benefits, if you need to, you can begin taking income when you turn 60. However, as with other benefit options, your monthly check will be permanently reduced for withdrawing benefits before FRA.

If your spouse began taking benefits before he or she died, you can't delay withdrawing your survivor's benefits to get delayed credits; the Social Security Administration says you can only get as much from a survivor's benefit as what your deceased spouse might have gotten, had he or she lived.[33]

Taxes, Taxes, Taxes

With Social Security, as with everything, it is important to consider taxes. It may be surprising, but your Social Security benefits are not tax-free. Despite having been

---

[33] Social Security Administration. 2017. "Social Security Benefit Amounts for The Surviving Spouse By Year Of Birth." https://www.ssa.gov/planners/survivors/survivorchartred.html. Accessed Jan. 11, 2017.

taxed to accrue those benefits in the first place, you may have to pay Uncle Sam income taxes on up to 85 percent of your Social Security.

The way the Social Security Administration figures these taxes is what they call the provisional income formula. Your provisional income formula differs from the adjusted gross income you use for your regular income taxes. Instead, to find out how much of your Social Security benefit is taxable, the Social Security Administration calculates it this way:

Provisional Income = Adjusted Gross Income + Nontaxable Interest + ½ of Social Security

See that piece about nontaxable interest? That generally means interest from government bonds and notes. It surprises many people that, although you may not pay taxes on those assets, their income will count against you when it comes to Social Security taxation.

Once you have figured out your provisional income (also called "combined income"), you can use the following chart to figure out your Social Security taxes.[34]

---

[34] Social Security Administration. 2017. "Benefits Planner: Income Taxes and Your Social Security Benefits." https://www.ssa.gov/planners/taxes.html. Accessed Jan. 26, 2017.

Taxes on Social Security		
Provisional Income = Adjusted Gross Income + Nontaxable Interest + ½ of Social Security		
If you are ___ and your provisional income is___, then...		Uncle Sam will tax ___ of your Social Security
Single	Married, filing jointly	
Less than $25,000	Less than $32,000	0%
$25,000 to $34,000	$32,000 to $44,000	Up to 50%
More than $34,000	More than $44,000	Up to 85%

This is one more reason it may be to your advantage to work with a financial professional: He or she can take a look at your entire picture to make your overall retirement plan as tax efficient as possible — including your Social Security benefit.

Clint and Bobbi arrived in my office confused and overwhelmed. I shared several options with them regarding when and how to file for the maximum Social Security benefit based on their unique situation. These will differ for each couple and single individual. I told them, "Social Security should be viewed as just one tool in the bag of options that must be considered when creating a retirement income plan."

Social Security will create a foundation or base income for them. At its maximum tax exposure, only 85 percent of the income from Social Security can be taxable as income, whereas income from an IRA or 401(k) will be 100 percent taxable as ordinary income, while dividends and capital gains income will usually enjoy a more preferred rate.

I explained that a tax nightmare can be created from a combination of all three of these sources of income and they can snowball into much higher marginal tax rate. For Clint and Bobbi, working in conjunction with their CPA would be key in providing a better chance to create a more tax-advantaged income plan.

With clients in this situation, I typically use a tax deferral strategy on non-retirement accounts to reduce the provisional income that triggers higher taxes on Social Security income. Mutual funds can create capital gains income even without liquidating the fund due to the fund's sale of assets positioned within the fund itself. We might also choose a more tax-preferred holding of exchange-traded funds, which have been known to have less capital gains tax exposure.

Working and Social Security: The Earnings Test

If you haven't reached FRA, but you started your Social Security benefits and are still working, things get a little hairy.

Because you have started Social Security payments, the Social Security Administration will pay out your benefits (docked, of course, for what you could have gotten if you had waited to file until your FRA). Yet, because you are working, the organization must also withhold from your check to add to your benefits ... which you are already collecting. See how this complicates matters?

To straighten the situation, the government has what is called the earnings test. For 2018, you can earn up to $17,040 without it affecting your Social Security check.

RETIREMENT, AKA UNEMPLOYMENT | 87

But for every $2 you earn past that amount, the Social Security Administration will withhold $1. The earnings test loosens in the year of your FRA; if you are reaching FRA in 2018, you can earn up to $45,360 before you run into the earnings test, and the government only withholds $1 for every $3 past that amount. The month you reach FRA, you are no longer subject to any earnings withholding. For instance, if you are still working and will turn 66 on July 17, 2019, you would only have to worry about the earnings test until July, and then you can ignore it entirely. Keep in mind, the money the government withholds from your Social Security benefits while you are working before FRA will be tacked back onto your benefits check after FRA.[35]

With all these options, making the decision of when to pull the trigger on Social Security can become quite complicated. I try to help my clients "look down the road" to see how the choices available under Social Security can affect their total income plan. Each couple or individual has so many variables to consider and each must have a clear picture of the potential long-term ramifications.

One couple may need to take the income more quickly to take pressure off their retirement funds, allowing for possible growth, while another couple may defer receiving benefits until their later years to ease some of the pressure on their assets later in life. A single person without heirs may wish to begin taking the benefit earlier, while the goal for a couple could be trying to wait as long as possible, possibly to age 70, to create a larger income base for the surviving spouse of the two.

---

[35] Social Security Administration. 2018. "Exempt Amounts Under the Earnings Test." https://www.ssa.gov/oact/cola/rtea.html. Accessed Feb. 16, 2018.

Through technological advancements in software programs and tools that perform in-depth analyses of a client's total financial picture, I have the ability to help people consider options that are right for their individual situation. I can merge those options into their income planning to consider not only Social Security as a stand-alone benefit, but also as something that can combine with their other income sources to create a composition of income that has the greatest probability for a stress-free retirement.

CHAPTER SIX

401(k)s & IRAs

H ave you heard? Today's retirement is not your dad's retirement. You see, back in the day, it was pretty common to work for one company for the vast majority of your career and then retire with a gold watch and a pension.

The gold watch was a symbol of the quality time you had put in at that company.

The pension was more than a symbol. Instead, it was a guarantee — as solid as your employer — that they would repay your hard work with a certain amount of income in your old age. Did you see that caveat there? Your pension's guarantee was *as solid as your employer*. The problem was, what if your employer went under?

Companies that failed couldn't pay their retired employees' pensions, leading to financial challenges for many. Beginning in 1974 with Congress' passage of the Employee Retirement Income Security Act, federal legislation and regulations aimed at protecting retirees were everywhere, including a relatively obscure section of the Internal Revenue Code, added in 1978. Section 401(k), to be specific.

IRC section 401, subsection k, created tax advantages for employer-sponsored financial products, even if the main contributor was the employee him or herself. Over the years, more employers took note, beginning an age of transition away from pensions and toward 401(k) plans. A 401(k) is a retirement account that has certain tax benefits and restrictions on the investments or other financial products inside of it.

Essentially, 401(k)s and their individual retirement account (IRA) counterparts are "wrappers" that provide tax benefits around other assets; typically the assets that compose IRAs and 401(k)s are mutual funds, stock and bond mixes, and money market accounts. However, IRA and 401(k) contents are becoming more diverse these days, with some companies offering different kinds of annuity options within their plans.

Where pensions are defined-*benefit* plans, 401(k)s and their individual retirement account (IRA) counterparts are defined-*contribution* plans. The one-word change outlines the basic difference. Pensions spell out what you can expect to receive from the plan, but not necessarily how much money it will take to fund those benefits. With 401(k)s, an employer sets a standard for how much they will contribute (if any), and you can be certain of what you are contributing, but there is no outline for what you can expect to receive in return for those contributions.

Modern employment looks very different these days. A 2014 survey determined that U.S. workers stayed with their employers a median of five years. Workers ages 55 to 64 had a little more staying power and were most likely to stay with their employer for about 10 years.[36] Additionally, in 1979, when those employees would have been hitting their strides, career-wise, 38 percent of workers had pensions. These days, it's closer to 13 percent of the

---

[36] Catalyst. Aug. 12, 2016. "Turnover and Retention." http://www.catalyst.org/knowledge/turnover-and-retention. Accessed Jan. 25, 2017.

workforce, while the number of those with defined-contribution plans has soared from 17 to 44 percent in the same period.[37]

A far cry from a pension and gold watch, wouldn't you say?

Those who have a pension face a different set of planning considerations than those without. While the planning process is not made more difficult, the addition of more income options does create more decisions that they will need to make.

The first area of consideration is how to take the income provided with a pension. For the single individual, the decision is very direct. They will take a single-life payout, which means they will receive income for their lifetime. A couple will usually be presented with several options to provide an income available to the survivor after the first to die. Spousal options will usually result in a lower income each month than choosing a single-life payout. A common option is joint-life, which is a reduced amount that will remain static throughout the lifetime of both lives. The options available to any individual will be as different as each pension.

An important note about taking pension income is the income is "irrevocable." That is a big word when we enter the financial arena, because you are making a choice that cannot be changed. You have decided upon a source of income that will come as ordinary income for the rest of your life. You cannot stop it, you cannot change it, and you cannot pass it to someone else.

-----

37 Employee Benefit Research Institute. "FAQs About Benefits — Retirement Issues."
https://www.ebri.org/publications/benfaq/index.cfm?fa=retfaq14.
Accessed Aug. 14, 2017.

Pensions can also have options such as cost-of-living adjustments (COLA) or even options to allow the pension funds to be rolled over to an IRA in lieu of taking a lifetime income payout.

Being clearly informed about all the different options is a must.

If there is anything to learn from this paradigm shift, it's that you have to look out for you. Whether you have worked for a company for two years or 20, you are still the one who has to look out for your own best interests. That holds doubly true when it comes to preparing for retirement. If you are one of the lucky ones who still has a pension, good for you. But for the rest of us, it is likely that a 401(k) — or possibly one of its nonprofit- or government-job counterparts, a 403(b) or 457 plan — is one of your biggest assets for retirement.

Some employers offer incentives to contribute to their company plans, like a company match. On that subject, I have one thing to say: DO IT! Nothing in life is free, as they say, but a company match on your retirement funds is about as close to free money as I think it gets. If you can make the minimum to qualify for your company's match at all, go for it.

Now, it's likely that during our working years, we mostly "set and forget" our 401(k) funding. Because it is tax-advantaged, your employer is taking money from your paycheck — before taxes — and putting it into your plan for you. Maybe you got to pick a selection of investments, or maybe your company only offers one choice of investment in your 401(k). Either way, while you are gainfully employed, your most impactful decision may just be the decision to continue funding your plan in the first place. But when you are ready to retire or move jobs, you have choices to make that require a little more thought and care.

When you are ready to part ways with your job, you have a few options:

- Leave the money where it is
- Take the cash (and pay income taxes and perhaps a 10% additional federal tax if you are younger than age 59 ½)
- Transfer the money to another employer plan (if the new plan allows)
- Roll the money over into a self-directed IRA

Now, these are just general options. You will have to decide, hopefully with the help of a financial professional, what's right for you. For instance, 401(k)s are typically pretty closely tied to the companies that offer them, so when changing jobs, it may not always be possible to transfer a 401(k) to another 401(k). Leaving the money where it is may also be out of the question — some companies have direct cash-out or rollover policies once someone is no longer employed.

Remember what we said earlier about how we change jobs more often these days? That means you likely have a 401(k) with your current company, but you may also have a string of IRAs trailing you from other jobs.

When Emma visited with me for our initial discovery meeting, she came in very prepared. She had copies of all her statements, accounts, policies and contracts. I will never forget having to get a second sheet of paper to list them all. Emma was a wonderful saver. Every year, she invested in an IRA as well as contributing to her 403(b) at the hospital where she worked. She had a total of four different 403(b)s from different jobs over the years and more than 15 different IRA accounts.

We helped her consolidate those accounts so she could see it all together clearly.

Organization can be a wonderful thing. It helps to focus your investment plan, track your returns and, most of all, not lose accounts. Yes, you heard correctly: lose accounts. Each state has a "lost fund" department or agency associated with lost or abandoned accounts, holding funds, just waiting for the rightful owner to claim their money. Organize and consolidate your accounts some rainy afternoon. Your money will thank you.

When it comes to your retirement income, it's important to be able to pull together ALL of your assets, so you can examine what you have and where.

Tax-Qualified, Tax-Preferred, Tax-Deferred ... Still TAXED

Financial media often cite IRAs and 401(k)s for their tax benefits. After all, with traditional plans, you put your money in, pre-tax, and it hopefully grows for years, even decades, untaxed. That's why these accounts are called tax-qualified or tax-deferred assets. They aren't TAX-FREE! Rarely does Uncle Sam allow business to go on without receiving his piece of the pie, and your retirement assets are no different. If you didn't pay taxes on the front end, you will pay taxes on the money you withdraw from these accounts in retirement. Don't get me wrong: This isn't an inherently bad thing, nor is it a good thing; it's just the way it is. It's important to understand, though, for the sake of planning ahead.

In retirement, many people assume they will be in a lower tax bracket. Are you planning to pare down your lifestyle in retirement? Perhaps you are, and perhaps you will have substantially less income in retirement. But many of my clients tell me they want to live life more or less the same as they always have. The money they would previously have spent on business attire or gas for their commute they now want to spend on hobbies and grandchildren. That's all fine, and for many of them, it is doable, but does it put them in a lower tax bracket? No.

Because of their special tax status, IRAs, 401(k)s and their alternatives have a few limitations that you should understand. For one thing, the IRS sets limits on your contributions to these retirement accounts. If you are contributing to a 401(k) or an equivalent nonprofit or government plan, your annual contribution limit is $18,500 (as of 2018). If you are 50 or older, the IRS allows additional contributions, called catch-up contributions, of up to $6,000 on top of the regular limit of $18,500. For an IRA, the limit is $5,500, with a catch-up limit of an additional $1,000.[38]

Because their tax advantages come from their intended use for retirement income, withdrawing funds from these accounts before you turn 59 ½ can carry stiff penalties. In addition to fees your investment management company might charge, you will have to pay income tax AND a 10 percent federal tax penalty.

---

[38] IRS. Oct. 19, 2017. "IRS Announces 2018 Pension Plan Limitations; 401(k) Contribution Limit Increases to $18,500 for 2018." https://www.irs.gov/newsroom/irs-announces-2018-pension-plan-limitations-401k-contribution-limit-increases-to-18500-for-2018. Accessed Feb. 8, 2018.

Now, there are a few exceptions to the 59 ½ rule:[39]

Exceptions to the 59 ½ Rule	
Exception	**Applies to IRA or 401(k)**
Death of account holder	Both
Total, permanent disability of account holder	Both
First-time homebuyer (up to $10,000)	IRA
Certain higher education expenses	IRA
Unreimbursed medical expenses up to a limit	IRA
Separation from employer service after age 55	401(k)

Other than the aforementioned exceptions, though, the 59 ½ rule for retirement accounts is incredibly important to remember, especially when you're young. Younger workers are often tempted to cash out an IRA from a previous employer and then are surprised to find their checks missing 20 percent of the account value to income taxes, penalty taxes and account fees.

---

[39] IRS. 2017. "Retirement Topics: Exceptions to Tax on Early Distributions." https://www.irs.gov/retirement-plans/plan-participant-employee/retirement-topics-tax-on-early-distributions. Accessed Feb. 8, 2017.

It's also important to keep in mind the 59 ½ rule for younger workers because many millennials I see in my practice come in and, while they may be socking money away in their workplace retirement plan, that is often the *only* place they are saving. This could be problematic later because of the 59 ½ rule; what if you have an emergency? It is important to fund your retirement, but you need to have some liquid assets handy as emergency funds. This can help you avoid breaking into your retirement accounts and incurring taxes and penalties as a result of the 59 ½ rule.

RMDs

Remember how we talked about the 401(k) or IRA being a "tax wrapper" for your funds? Well, eventually, Uncle Sam will want a bite of that candy bar. So, another condition of these accounts is that, beginning at 70 ½, the government requires you to withdraw a portion of your account, which they calculate based on the size of your account and your estimated lifespan. This required minimum distribution — or RMD — is the government's insurance that they will at some point get some taxes from your earnings. Because you didn't pay taxes on the front end, you will now pay income taxes on whatever you withdraw, including your RMDs. ALSO, let me just remind you not to play chicken with the U.S. government; if you don't take your RMDs starting at 70 ½, you will have to write a check to the IRS for 50 PERCENT of the amount of your missed RMDs.

Roth

Since the Taxpayer Relief Act of 1997, there has been a different kind of retirement account, or "tax wrapper," available to the public: the Roth. Roth IRAs and Roth 401(k)s each differ from their traditional counterparts in one big way, which is that you pay your taxes on the front end. This means once your post-tax money is in the Roth account, as long as you follow the rules and limitations of that account, your distributions are truly tax-free. You won't pay income tax when you take withdrawals, so, in turn, you don't have to worry about RMDs.

How would you like to have 20 to 25 percent more money in retirement? Who wouldn't, right? That's the potential advantage of a Roth IRA. As I have explained, every dollar you withdraw from an IRA, 401(k), or 403(b) is taxed as ordinary income. If you think you have a $200,000 IRA, in a way, you don't; the tax man is going to take a share, and based upon your other income, that account might only realistically represent $160,000 to $180,000. If you have a $500,000 IRA, you may have $400,000 to $425,000. Each person's tax liability will be different. With the Roth IRA, you pay your taxes prior to making a contribution and grow a tax-free bucket of money. This can be extremely valuable in the face of increasing inflation, which, when combined with unknown future tax rates, could diminish your purchasing power.

Since we are dealing with "after-tax" money that flows into the Roth IRA, it is important that we take a minute to talk about the ways you can fund this financial instrument.

First, you can contribute to a Roth account each year. Those contributions must be made each year by April 15 for the previous tax year, just like a traditional IRA. Likewise, if available at your employer, you can contribute to a Roth 401(k) by following the contribution limits based upon your age and allowable contribution level.

Secondly, you can convert other qualified retirement accounts into the Roth IRA. To do this, you will create a

Roth IRA and transfer funds into the account, say from an IRA. But there is one very important difference compared to contribution, you must pay the tax due on the converted funds as income. The decision to do this requires you to determine how much additional tax you are willing to pay to make this conversion. There are no limits; it's just about how much tax are you willing to pay. We do suggest and remind our clients to use every deduction available to them annually to reduce taxes or, in this case, offset taxes due on the conversion. Any conversion to a Roth IRA must be completed by Dec. 31 of the current tax year.

Converting a traditional IRA or qualified plan assets to a Roth IRA is a taxable event and could result in additional impacts on your personal tax situation, including a need for additional tax withholding or estimated tax payments, the loss of certain tax deductions and credits, and higher taxes on Social Security benefits and Medicare premiums. It is generally preferable that you have funds to pay the taxes due upon conversion from funds outside of your IRA or qualified plan. If you elect to take a distribution from your IRA or qualified plan to pay the conversion taxes, please keep in mind the potential consequences, such as an assessment of product surrender charges or additional IRS penalties for premature distributions.

Taking Charge

As mentioned earlier, the 401(k) and IRA have largely replaced pensions, but they aren't an equal trade.

Pensions are employer-funded; the money that goes into them is money that wouldn't ever show up on your pay stub. Because 401(k)s are self-funded, you have to actively and consciously save. This distinction has made a difference when it comes to funding retirement. As one source says:[40]

> "*$18,433. That's the median amount in a 401(k) savings account, according to a recent report by the Employee Benefit Research Institute. Almost 40 percent of employees have less than $10,000, even as the proportion of companies offering alternatives like defined benefit pensions continues to drop.*
>
> *"Older workers do tend to have more savings. At Vanguard, for example, the median for savers aged 55 to 64 in 2013 was $76,381. But even at that level, millions of workers nearing retirement are on track to leave the workforce with savings that do not even approach what they will need for health care, let alone daily living. Not surprisingly, retirement is now Americans' top financial worry, according to a recent Gallup poll.*"

While the piece cites many reasons people underfund their retirement plans, like being overwhelmed by the investment choices or taking withdrawals from IRAs when they leave an employer, the reason at the top of the list is this: People just aren't participating to begin with.

So, whether you have a 401(k) with an employer or have to have an IRA alternative with a private company, separate from your workplace, the most important retirement savings decision you can make is to sock away your money in the first place.

---

[40] Kelley Holland. CNBC Personal Finance. March 23, 2015. "For millions, 401(k) plans have fallen short." http://www.cnbc.com/2015/03/20/l-it-the-401k-is-a-failure.html. Accessed Feb. 8, 2017.

CHAPTER SEVEN

Annuities

In my practice, I offer my clients a variety of products, from securities to insurance, all designed to help them reach their financial goals. You may be wondering: Why single out a single product in this book?

Well, while most of my clients have a pretty good understanding of business and finance, I sometimes find those who have the impression there must be magic involved. Like turning straw into gold, or like Jack and the Beanstalk going from a cow to a bean to a sack of gold, a harp and a goose that lays golden eggs, some people assume there is a magic finance wand we can wave to change years' worth of savings into a strategy for retirement income.

Yet, finances aren't magic; it takes lots of hard work and, typically, several financial products and strategies to pull together a complete retirement plan. Of all the financial products I work with, it seems people find none more mysterious than annuities. And, if I may say, even some of those who recognize the word "annuity" have a limited understanding of the product. So, in the interest of demystifying annuities, let me tell you a little about what an annuity is.

Generally speaking, insurance is a financial hedge against risk. Car owners buy auto insurance to protect their finances in case they injure someone or someone injures them. Homeowners have house insurance to protect their finances in case of a fire, flood or another disaster. People also have life insurance to protect their finances in case of untimely death. Almost juxtaposed to life insurance, people have annuities in case of a long life; by providing consistent and reliable income payments, annuities can help with financial protection.

The basic premise of an annuity is that you, the annuitant, pay an insurance company some amount in exchange for their contractual guarantee that they will pay you income for a certain period of time. How that company pays you, for how long and how much are determined by the annuity contract you enter into with the insurance company.

How You Get Paid

There are two ways for an annuity contract to provide income: The first is through what is called annuitization, and the second is through the use of income riders. We'll get into income riders in a bit, but let's talk about annuitization. That nice, long word is, in my opinion, one reason annuities have a reputation for mystery and misinformation.

Annuitization

When someone "annuitizes" a contract, it is the point where he or she turns on the income stream. Once a contract has been annuitized, there is no going back. If the policyholder lives longer than the insurance company planned, the insurance company is still obligated to pay him or her, even if the payments end up being way more than the contract's actual value. If, however, the policyholder dies an untimely death, depending on the contract type, the insurance company may keep anything left of the money that funded the annuity — nothing would be paid out to the contract holder's survivors. You see where that could make some people balk?

At a high level, here's how it looks from the insurance company's side: Imagine the company has a "pie" of 10 people, who all buy contracts at the same time. In the beginning, 10 people receive income paid out by the company. A few, let's say three, die earlier on. Their remaining contract values are pooled back into the rest of the insurance company's pie. As the others age, they too die, many of them breaking even, with their pieces of the pie reaching zero around the time they pass away. One or two people even live well past the others, and, by the time they pass away, they have long since hit zero on the values of their contracts. The insurance company was still able to pay them their contractually agreed income using the money left in the pie, pooled from the two or three who passed away much earlier.

Now, I use this pie illustration as a way to show you the original concept of annuitization and how it works, from the perspectives of both an insurer and a contract holder. Modern annuities have so many bells and whistles that the picture I just described seems too simplified to do them justice, but it's important to at least have a basic concept of annuitization.

Riders

Remember what I said about bells and whistles? Modern annuities have a lot of different options these days, many in the form of riders that you can add to your contract for a fee — usually about 1 percent of the contract value per year. Each rider has its particularities, and the types of riders available will vary by the type of annuity contract purchased, but just to outline some of these little extras:

- Lifetime income rider: Contract guarantees you an enhanced income for life
- Death benefit rider: Contract pays an enhanced death benefit to your beneficiaries even if you have annuitized
- Return of premium rider: Guarantees that you (or your beneficiaries) will at least receive back the premium value of the annuity
- Long-term care rider: Provides a certain amount, sometimes as much as twice the principal value of the contract, to help pay for long-term care if the contract holder is moved to a nursing home or assisted living situation

This isn't an extensive look, and usually the riders have fancier names based on the issuing company, like Lorem Ipsum Insurance Company Income Preferred Bonus Fixed Index Annuity rider, but I just wanted to show you what some of the general options are in layman's terms.

Types of Annuities

Annuities break down into four basic types: immediate, variable, fixed and fixed index.

Immediate

Immediate annuities are not terribly popular because they primarily rely on annuitization to provide income — you give the insurance company a lump sum upfront, and your payments begin immediately. Once you begin receiving income payments, the transaction is irreversible and you no longer have access to your money in a lump sum. When you die, any remaining contract value is forfeited to the insurance company.

All other annuity contract types are "deferred" contracts, meaning you fund your policy as a lump sum or over a period of years and you give it the opportunity to grow over time — sometimes years, sometimes decades.

Variable

A variable annuity is an insurance contract wrapped around an investment. It's sold by insurance companies, but only through someone who is registered to sell investment products. With a variable annuity contract, the insurance company invests your money in the stock market. This makes it a bit different from the other annuity contract types because it is the only contract where your money is subject to losses as a result of market declines. Your contract value has a greater opportunity to grow, but it also stands to lose. Additionally, your contract's value will be subject to the underlying investment's fees and limitations — including capital gains taxes, management fees, etc. Once it is time for you to receive income from the contract, the insurance company will pay you a certain income, locked in at whatever your contract's value was.

Let's address the fees associated with the variable annuity and their effect on income from that annuity.

There are several common types of fees that compose the cost of ownership of this type of annuity. While some are standard, others are optional, much like the rider fee previously illuminated. Over the years, we have evaluated hundreds of variable annuities with different levels of fees, each as different as the product. In general, we have seen fees range from as low as 0.50 percent to as high as 3.50 percent.

Since the variable annuity is invested in mutual fund holdings, the value can go up and down based upon market returns and volatility. Those mutual funds will each have a fee composed of several smaller fees called fund fees. These fees are associated with the operation of the mutual fund and are identical to those found in brokerage accounts and at mutual fund companies.

A mortality and expense fee provides that a death benefit will be paid based upon a guaranteed value should a death occur while the value of the contract is diminished or down due to a market correction, In essence, the owner is purchasing life insurance to protect themselves in case the value drops.

An administrative fee is also common and is exactly as the name implies.

At times, optional riders may be added to the base contract for an additional charge. A death benefit rider may be available to enhance the death benefit and can actually increase the benefit over time relative to some schedule. An income rider may be added at the option of the owner to provide some form of income payout guarantee in the future.

When taking income from the variable annuity, your considerations for the pressure that fees can place on the funds must be considered. For example, let's assume you have $100,000 invested in a variable annuity. You need to withdraw 4 percent this year for income. Let's also assume the fees for this product are 3 percent. Then, the effective withdrawal from the account this year would be 7 percent, or $7,000. Of course, this is no different than any account with a fee of 3 percent, but the pull-down may be exceeding safe levels to provide for the longevity of this account.

Imagine, as with the required minimum distribution with an IRA, that you had to withdraw an increasing percentage of your account value each year for income. The long-term viability of the account can easily come into concern.

Manage your fees, no matter what the account type, as they will reduce the real money that the investment can put into your hands. Furthermore, by reducing your fees, you can increase your yield or income, if needed — more money in your hands is what retirement income is all about.

Fixed

A traditional fixed annuity is pretty straightforward. You purchase a contract with a guaranteed interest rate and, when you are ready, the insurance company will make regular income payments to you at whatever payout rate your contract guarantees. Those payments will continue for the rest of your life and, if you choose, for the remainder of your spouse's life.

Fixed annuities don't have much in the way of upside potential, but many people like them for their guarantees (after all, if your Aunt May lived to be 95, knowing you have a paycheck later in life can be a mental and financial safety net) as well as for their predictability. Unlike variable annuities, which are subject to market risk and might be up one year and down the next, you can pretty well calculate the value of your fixed annuity over your lifetime.

Fixed Index

To recap, variable annuities take on more risk to offer more possibilities to grow. Fixed annuities have less potential growth, but they protect your principal. In the last couple of decades, many insurance companies have retooled their product line to offer fixed index annuities, which are sort of midway between variable and fixed annuities on that risk/reward spectrum. Fixed index annuities offer greater growth potential than traditional fixed annuities but less than variable annuities. Like traditional fixed annuities, however, fixed index annuities are protected from downside market losses.

Fixed index annuities are market-linked contracts, meaning that, instead of your contract value growing at a set interest rate like a traditional fixed annuity, it has the potential to grow within a range. Your contract's value is credited interest based on the performance of an external market index like the S&P 500. You can't invest in the S&P 500 directly, but the insurance company will credit your annuity contract based on the S&P 500's gains, up to a cap. For instance, if your contract caps your interest at 5 percent, then in a year that the S&P 500 gains 3 percent, your annuity value increases 3 percent. If the S&P 500 gains 35 percent, your annuity value gets a 5 percent bump. But since your money isn't actually invested in the market with a fixed index annuity, if the market nosedives (2000 and 2008, anyone?), you won't see any increase in your contract value. Conversely, there will also be no decrease in your contract value—no matter how badly the market performed, you won't lose any of the interest you were credited in previous years.

So, what if the S&P 500 shows a market loss of 30 percent? Your contract value isn't going anywhere. For those who are more interested in protection than growth potential, fixed index annuities can be an attractive option because, when the stock market has a long period of positive performance, a fixed index annuity will enjoy a conservative gain in its value that usually has more upside potential than just offsetting the effects of inflation. And during stretches where the stock market is erratic, and stock values across the board take significant losses? Fixed index annuities won't lose anything from the stock market volatility.

Perspective with every financial product is paramount. We must identify the true purpose of the fixed index annuity and why we might allocate a portion of our assets to this product.

Over the years, as we invest, we hold some amount of our assets in both market risk positions and others in what is like a counterbalance of safer holdings, with the amounts that we allocate to each being based upon our individual feeling of risk or fear of loss due to risk. This may be expressed in a 60/40 holding of growth-positioned assets and assets in bond positions. Or maybe it's 70/30. There are many different combinations, as you might imagine. As we age, we can ill afford to have losses that might affect our ability to provide for our income needs when we can no longer work to create income. In other words, we need to hold some of our retirement funds where they are not exposed to the possibility of market risk and loss. However, the dilemma with what we might call "safe money" is how to get higher returns.

The purpose of the fixed index annuity is to seek higher rates of interest on money that is protected from downside market risk. This is important to understand without any confusion. The fixed index annuity cannot compare with actual market investments, which are exposed to market risk and have unlimited growth potential. It is designed to provide interest earnings higher than can typically be achieved with other financial products that are also protected from downside market risk, so a fixed index annuity may provide more interest earnings than other forms of insurance-based products. Its value cannot decrease due to market or index losses, and that protection provides a form of "sleep insurance" for those who no longer can feel comfortable with the roller coaster ride of volatility.

Other Things to Know About Annuities

We just talked about the four different kinds of annuity contracts available, but all of them have some commonalities as annuities.

For all annuities, the contractual guarantees are only as strong as the insurance company that sells the product, which makes it important to thoroughly check the credit ratings of any company whose products you are considering.

Annuities are tax-deferred, meaning you don't have to pay taxes upfront and on interest earnings as the contract value grows. Instead, you will pay ordinary income taxes on your withdrawals. These are meant to be long-term products, so, similar to other tax-deferred or tax-advantaged products, if you begin taking withdrawals from your contract before age 59 ½, you may have to pay a 10 percent federal tax penalty. Also, while annuities are generally considered illiquid, most contracts allow you to withdraw up to 10 percent of your contract value every year, but more than that and you could incur penalties. Keep in mind, your withdrawals will deplete the accumulated cash value, death benefit and possibly the rider values of your contract.

The fixed annuity is a financial tool that can serve an important role in many different financial planning strategies, which make it feasible for consideration.

Generally speaking, because of the aforementioned qualities (it has a low-dollar purchase threshold, liquidity up to 10 percent annually for most contracts, various time holding periods, several different income options, tax deferral, and guarantees based upon the financial strength of the insurance company) fixed annuities can be useful as a product anchor in a number of income strategies.

The lack of liquidity must always be evaluated when considering any annuity. You should never place funds needed for liquidity in any instrument that has a time structure that may limit access to needed funds. This also holds true for certificates of deposit, bonds, and some mutual funds with liquidation expenses.

Using a bucket strategy, we can segment assets such as fixed annuities to be used at a time when needed for income. A laddering technique, much like we do with bonds or certificates of deposit, can provide liquidity at the right time, where we know when and how much is needed to meet an expense or shift to an income strategy.

Annuities aren't for everyone, but it's important to understand them before saying "yea" or "nay" on whether they fit in your plan; otherwise you're not operating with complete information, wouldn't you agree? Regardless, you should talk to a financial professional who can help you understand annuities, help you dissect your particular financial needs and show you whether an annuity is appropriate for your retirement income plan.

CHAPTER EIGHT

Health Care

Given that health care has been one of the favorite bargaining chips of the past few U.S. presidential administrations, there's no telling what changes Congress could enact during the 20- to 30-year period you could spend in retirement. I think my eyes are going to glaze over if I read one more "what if" on the subject. Yet, this is just one of the many reasons health care and its related costs are some of the biggest nail-biters of retirement.

At Barnard Financial Group, we don't have a government affiliation, we aren't working with a state agency and we don't get to set health policy. But we help our clients navigate these systems and plan for ways to fund health emergencies and care in retirement. If you want to get down to the nitty-gritty of Medicare and Medicaid and stay up to date on whatever state and federal rules are in place, you can check out www.Medicare.gov and www.Medicaid.gov. Here, though, I'd like to give a general idea of the considerations each of us will face when it comes to paying for health care.

Retiring Early

A big part of planning for retirement revolves around retirement income. After all, retirement is cutting the cord that tethers you to your employer — and your monthly check. However, that check also comes with many other benefits, particularly health care. Health care is often unexpectedly the thing that puts dreams for an early retirement on hold. Some employers offer health benefits to their retired workers, but that number has declined drastically over the past several decades. In 1988, among employers who offered health benefits to their workers, 66 percent offered health benefits to their retirees. In 2016, that number was 24 percent.[41]

So, with employer-offered retirement health benefits on the wane, this becomes a big point of concern for anyone who is looking to retire, particularly those who are looking to retire before age 65, when they would become eligible for Medicare coverage. In 2014, Fidelity Investments estimated the average couple who retires at 62 could expect to spend $17,000 a year in out-of-pocket health care costs until they enroll in Medicare.[42] Again, that was in 2014. Do you think it's likely that cost went down?

Even if you are working until 65 or have plans to cover your health expenses until that point, I often have clients who incorrectly assume that Medicare is their golden

[41] Henry J. Kaiser Family Foundation. Sept. 14, 2016. "2016 Employer Health Benefits Survey Section Eleven: Retiree Health Benefits." http://kff.org/report-section/ehbs-2016-section-eleven-retiree-health-benefits/. Accessed Aug. 15, 2017.

[42] Susan B. Garland. Kiplinger. June 13, 2014. "A Reality Check on Health Care Costs for Early Retirees." http://www.kiplinger.com/article/retirement/T027-C022-S003-reality-check-health-care-costs-early-retirees.html. Accessed Aug. 15, 2017.

ticket, that it will cover all expenses. That is simply not the case.

Medicare

So, once you're 65, if you have paid into the system for at least 10 years, you are eligible for Medicare enrollment. You can enroll in Medicare anytime during the three months before and four months after your 65th birthday. Miss your enrollment deadline, and you could risk paying increased premiums for the rest of your life. On top of prompt enrollment, there are a few other things to think about when it comes to Medicare, not least among them the need to understand the different "parts," what they do and what they don't.

Part A

Medicare Part A is what you might think of as "classic" Medicare. Hospital care, some types of home health care and major medical care fall under this. While most enrollees pay nothing for this service (as they likely paid into the system for at least 10 years), you may end up paying, either based on work history or delayed sign-up. In 2018, the highest premium is $422 per month, and a hospital stay does have a deductible, $1,340.[43] And, if you have a hospital stay that surpasses 60 days, you could be looking at additional costs; keep in mind that Medicare doesn't pay for long-term care and services.

---

[43] Medicare. 2018. "Medicare 2018 Costs at a Glance." https://www.medicare.gov/your-medicare-costs/costs-at-a-glance/costs-at-glance.html. Accessed Feb 10, 2018.

Part B

Medicare Part B is a pretty much essential piece of wrap-around coverage for Medicare Part A. It helps pay for doctor's visits and outpatient services. This also comes with a price tag: Although the Part B deductible is only $183 in 2018, you will still pay 20 percent of all costs after that, with no limit on out-of-pocket expenses.[44]

Part C

Medicare Part C, more commonly known as Medicare Advantage plans, are an alternative to a combination of Parts A, B and sometimes D. Administered through private insurance companies, these have a variety of costs and restrictions and are subject to the specific policies and rules of the issuing carrier.

Part D

Medicare Part D is also through a private insurer and is supplemental to Parts A and B as its primary purpose is to cover prescription drugs. Like any private insurance plan, Part D has its quirks and rules that vary from insurer to insurer.

The Donut Hole

Even with a "Part D" in place, you may still have a coverage gap between what your Part D private drug insurance pays for your prescription and what basic Medicare pays. In 2018, the coverage gap is $3,750, meaning that after you meet your private prescription insurance limit, you will spend $3,750 out of pocket (not including any copays or cost shares that you paid before

---

[44] Ibid.

meeting the limit!) before Medicare will kick in to pay for more prescription drugs.

Med Sup

Medicare Supplemental Insurance, MedSup, Medigap, or plans that are labeled Medicare Part F, G, H, I, J... Known by a variety of monikers, this is just a fancy way of saying "medical coverage for those over 65 that picks up the tab for whatever the federal Medicare program(s) doesn't." Again, costs, limitations, etc. vary by carrier.

Does that sound like a bunch of government alphabet soup to you? It certainly does to me. And, did you read that fine print? Unpredictable costs, varied restrictions, difficult-to-compare benefits, donut holes and coverage gaps. That's par for the course with health care plans through the course of our adult lives. What gives? I thought Medicare was supposed to be easier, comprehensive, at no cost!

The truth is there is no stage of life at which health care is easy to understand.

Mistakes abound in this arena, and you need a professional who can outline your areas of exposure. I have witnessed those who did not cover the 20 percent amount not paid by Medicare and have seen enormous health care costs completely decimate their retirement savings, while others created penalty situations for themselves by not filing for coverage, whether for Part D or for Medicare itself, in a timely manner.

Bruce visited with my firm with questions about Social Security and reaching his full retirement age. While learning more about him, I inquired about his signing up for Medicare back at age 65. He gave me a blank look, shrugged his shoulders and said, "Oh, no." A mistake like this can cost thousands of dollars if the right — or maybe I should say the wrong — situation occurs. You must sign up at age 65 for Medicare. There is a very important period of seven months, beginning three months before you reach 65 and four months after. If you do not sign up during this time period, you could pay higher premiums for the rest of your life.

It is easy to become complacent as you move toward that retirement goal you have worked for. Yet, as you approach this date, continuing education is as important as ever. You must make decisions in a timely manner. One common mistake we see is that, while an individual has learned to take care of themselves, in a couple, often only one person manages the money and pays the bills. Both members of a couple need to be engaged because, at some point, the couple will decrease to being one individual. That individual has to have knowledge of their financial situation and how to move forward.

As I have expressed previously, build a network of trusted advisors and counselors that you can go to for help and information.

The best thing you can do for yourself is to scope out the health care field early, compare costs often and prepare for out-of-pocket costs well in advance — decades, if possible.

LTC

Now, I know we cover longevity and the costs of long-term care elsewhere in this book, but it is so incredibly important and often overlooked that some pieces will bear repeating.

- The longer you live, the more likely you are to continue living, and the longer you live, the more health care you need to pay for.

- The average cost of a private nursing home in the United States in 2016 was $7,698 a month.[45] But keep in mind, that is just the nursing home — that doesn't include other medical costs, let alone the pleasantries like entertainment or hobby spending.
- In 2015, HealthView Services and Fidelity calculated that a healthy couple retiring at age 65 would pay around $250,000 over the course of retirement just for Medicare and wraparound coverage premiums.
- Women will need, on average, $22,000 more than men.[46]

I know. Whoa there, Jeff, I was hoping to have a realistic idea of health costs, not be driven over by a cement mixer!

The good news is that, while we don't know these exact costs in advance, we know there *will* be costs. And you won't have to pay your total Medicare lifetime premiums in one day as a lump sum. Now that you have a good idea of health care costs in retirement, you can PLAN for them! That's the real point, here: Planning in advance can keep you from feeling nickel-and-dimed to your wits' end. Instead, having a sizeable portion of your assets earmarked for health care can give you the freedom to choose health care networks, coverage options and long-term care spaces that you like and that you think offer you the best of life.

[45] Genworth Financial. April 2016. "Genworth 2016 Cost of Care Survey." https://www.genworth.com/about-us/industry-expertise/cost-of-care.html. Accessed Feb. 23, 2017.

[46] Katie Lobosco. CNN Money. Dec. 30, 2015. "Don't Freak Out About Health Care Costs in Retirement." http://money.cnn.com/2015/12/30/retirement/retirement-health-care-costs/. Accessed Feb. 23, 2017.

Those who have witnessed parents or a family member walk through the health care expenses of aging usually become the best prepared to face that process themselves. While long-term care expenses can erode an estate, the advanced preparation for expenses that can manifest over 15 to 20 years of retirement, leading up to possibly a higher level of care, requires attention. These expenses can be even more devastating to a couple than an individual. Those precious retirement dollars must be counted on to provide supplemental income in addition to Social Security for two people for many years and then be sufficient to provide for the survivor, after the first in a couple dies. With the reduction in income upon the loss of a spouse, health care expenses for the remaining spouse — not to mention care in an assisted living or nursing home — can wreak financial havoc on an estate. Loss of options as we approach the care-need phase of life limits the quality of care available to us.

Frank was able to enjoy time with his mother during the years after the death of his father. She remained in her home until her care needs required that she move into an assisted living community. For three years, she enjoyed care from doctor visits and, eventually, from the daily assistance of caregivers in the community. For Frank, there was a comfort in his knowing she had all she needed until her death. Moreover, he was able to visit her and enjoy their time together without worrying about her being alone when he was out of town on business. All of this was possible because he had taken the initiative to purchase a long-term care insurance policy for his mom after the death of this father. One of the first things he wanted after she passed was a policy for him and his wife, not because of fear, but for the assurance that they would have care options available to them in the future and would be able to live life on their terms.

CHAPTER NINE

Estate & Legacy

I n my practice, I devote a significant portion of my time to matters of estates. That doesn't mean drawing up wills or trusts or putting together powers of attorney or anything like that. After all, I'm not an estate planning attorney. But I am a financial professional, and what part of the "estate" isn't affected by money matters?

I've included this chapter because I have seen people do it wrong. Clients, or clients' families, have come in after having had a death in the family and have found themselves in the middle of probate, or high taxes, or have discovered that something unforeseen (often long-term care) drained the estate.

Alternately, I have seen people do it right: clients or families who visit my office to talk about legacies and how to make them last, adult children who have room to grieve without an added burden of unintended costs, without stress from a family ruptured because of inadequate planning.

I will share some of those stories here, not to give specific advice (obviously you have unique circumstances and will need the help of an attorney to be sure your wishes are carried out), but to give you some things to think about and to underscore the importance of planning ahead.

My firm has always and will continue to maintain partnerships with both CPAs and estate planning attorneys. During our financial planning process, we drill down into both what clients currently have in the way of legal documents and what might be needed. I then can direct them to a source capable of meeting that need. The assessment or discovery process with a financial advisor may be less intimidating than going through the same process with an attorney. While one person might need advanced estate planning to the tune of a trust or elevated charitable planning, another may need only a simple will or durable financial power of attorney.

You Can't Take It With You

When it comes to legacy and estate planning, the most important thing is to DO IT. I have heard people from clients to celebrities (national rap artist Snoop Dog/Lion comes to mind) who say they aren't interested in what happens to their assets when they die because they'll be dead. That's certainly one way to look at it. But I think that's a very selfish way to go about things — we all have people and causes we care about, not to mention those who care about us. Even if the people we love don't *need* what we leave behind, they can still be fined or legally tied up in the probate process or burial costs if we don't plan for those. And that's not even considering what happens if you become incapacitated at some point while you are still alive. Having a plan in place can greatly reduce the stress of those responsibilities on your loved ones; it's just a loving thing to do.

Documents

There are a few documents that lay the groundwork of legacy planning. You've probably heard of all or most of them, but I'd like to review what they are and how people commonly use them. These are all things you should talk about with an estate planning attorney to establish your legacy.

Powers of Attorney

A power of attorney is a document that gives someone the authority to act on your behalf, in your best interests. These come in handy in situations where you cannot be present (think, vacation where you get stuck in Canada) or, for durable powers of attorney, even when you are incapacitated (think, in a coma or coping with dementia).

It is important to have powers of attorney in place and to appoint someone you trust to act on your behalf in these matters. Have you ever heard of someone who was incapacitated after a car accident, whether from head trauma or being in a coma for weeks — sometimes months? Do you think their bills stopped coming due during that time? I like my phone company and my bank, but neither one is about to put a moratorium on sending me bills, particularly not for an extended and interminable period. A power of attorney, or POA, would have the authority to make sure your mortgage gets paid or cancel your cable while you are unable to.

***You can have multiple POAs
and require them to act jointly.***

What this looks like: Do you think two heads are better than one? One man, Chris, greatly relied on his two sons' opinions for both his business and personal matters. He appointed both sons as joint POA, requiring both their signoffs for his medical and financial matters.

You can have multiple POAs who can act independently.

What this looks like: Irene had three children with whom she routinely stayed. They lived in different areas of the country, which she thought was an advantage; one month she might be hiking out West, the next she could enjoy the newest off-Broadway production and the next she could soak up some Southern sun. She named her three children as independently authorized POAs so, if something happened, no matter where she was, the child closest could step in to act on her behalf.

You can have POAs who have different responsibilities.

What this looks like: Although Luke's friend Claire, a nurse, was his go-to and POA for health-related issues, financial matters usually made her nervous, so he appointed his good neighbor, Matt, as his POA in all of his financial and legal matters.

In addition to POAs, it may be helpful to have an advanced medical directive. This is a document where you have pre-decided what choices you would make about different health scenarios. An advanced medical directive can help ease the burden for your medical POA and loved ones, particularly when it comes to end-of-life care.

I can't overstate how important these documents are in your planning process. Occasionally, we hear on the national stage of a person, usually a celebrity, whose life has collided with a need for the power of attorney. When you need it, but do not have it, you or your family members have a problem.

"Who will speak for you when you cannot," is a question we ask every individual or couple we meet. Back in 2013, I interviewed a gentleman who had been referred to us by a health care worker. His mother was in the hospital. He explained that, earlier in the week, during the night, she had a health scare and somehow had driven herself to the hospital. She was disoriented and found wandering the halls at 3 a.m. The doctor who treated her declared she was incompetent due to a dementia diagnosis. Since she did not have either of the powers of attorney that allowed someone to make her financial or health care decisions on her behalf, and now had been declared incompetent, she would be unable to create those documents. She also did not have a will. The family had to endure the cost of what we call "living probate" to have guardians appointed for her. The family now had to submit to annual evaluations and be scrutinized over the decisions they are making on her behalf in both providing her care and spending her money for her care.

These simple documents can make a difficult situation much easier on those who must care for you.

Wills

Perhaps the most basic document of legacy planning, a will is a legal document wherein you outline your wishes for your estate. When it comes to your estate after your death, having a will is the foundation of your legacy. Without one, your loved ones are left behind, guessing what you would have wanted, and the court will largely split your assets according to whatever the state's defaults are. And maybe that's exactly what you wanted, as far as anyone knows, right? Because even if you told your nephew that he could have your car he's been driving, if it's not in writing, it still might go to the brother, sister, son or daughter to whom you aren't talking.

However, it may not be enough just to have a will. Even with a will, your assets will be subject to probate. Probate is what we call the state's process for determining a will's validity. A judge will go through your will to question if it is in conflict with state law, if it is the most up-to-date document, if you were mentally competent at the time it was in order, etc. For some, this is a quick, easily resolved process. For others, particularly if someone steps forward to contest the will, it may take years to settle, all the while subjecting their assets to court costs and attorney's fees.

One other undesirable piece of the probate process is that it is a public process. That means anyone can go to the courthouse, ask for copies of the case and find out your assets, as well as who is slated to receive what and who is disputing.

If you ever listened to pop music, the name Prince is not foreign to you. Prince died in 2016 with an estate valued at more than $200 million dollars, with no will. The probate court will decide where those dollars go, and at significant cost to the estate. This mistake is more common than you might imagine.

I feel many people have a fear of sitting with an advisor or attorney and opening up their lives to the questions and answers that are necessary to create a document that will clarify how they want their belongings and assets to be distributed at their death. I see the anxiousness on the face of many as we talk. I have had many state, "Well, I am going to be dead, it will get figured out." While it will eventually get figured out, the public nature of the process and the fact that probate can take months or years, with exposure to anyone who visits the courthouse, can be much more invasive for their family, estate representative, and reputation of the deceased — and that's not to mention the additional cost.

It's also important to remember that beneficiary lines trump wills. So, that large life insurance policy? What if, when you bought it 15 years ago, you wrote your ex-husband's name on the beneficiary line? Even if you stipulate otherwise in your will, the company that holds your policy will pay out to your ex-spouse. Or, how about the thousands of dollars in your IRA you dedicated to "children" 30 years ago, but one of your children was killed in a car accident, leaving his wife and two toddlers behind? That IRA is going to transfer to your remaining children, with nothing for your daughter-in-law and grandchildren.

That may paint a grim portrait, but I can't underscore enough the importance of working with a skilled estate planning attorney to keep your will and beneficiary lines up to date as your life changes for the sake of your loved ones.

While beneficiary designations can create problems, they can also be used to avoid the probate process, as accounts that list designated beneficiaries do not go through probate. Beneficiary designations are private and can only be disclosed to the beneficiary. For those who want complete control and absolutely know where they want proceeds to pass, this can be a significant advantage.

A close family friend lost her mother a few years back. In the process of remarrying after a divorce, her mother neglected to change the will and, upon her death, the proceeds were left to the ex-husband. To complicate the mistake, the ex-husband had developed dementia and, since he was not cognitive, could not represent himself. It took two years to resolve the issue, which did not end favorably for our friend.

An annual review of your beneficiary designations is important. Situations change and you need to be sure that *your wishes* are honored.

Trusts

Another piece of legacy planning to consider is the trust.

A trust is set up through an attorney and allows a third party, or trustee, to hold your assets and determine how they will pass to your beneficiaries. Many people are skeptical of trusts because they assume trusts are only appropriate for the fabulously wealthy.

However, a simple trust may only cost $1,600 to $3,000 in attorney's fees[47] and can avoid both the expense and publicity of probate, provide a more immediate transfer of wealth, avoid some taxes and provide you greater control of your legacy.

For instance, if you want to set aside some funds for a grandchild's college education, you can make it a requirement that he or she enrolls in classes before your trust will dispense any funds. Like a will, beneficiary lines will override your trust conditions, so you must still keep insurance policies and other assets up to date.

Like any financial or legal consideration, there are many options these days beyond the yes/no of having a trust. For one thing, you will need to consider if you want your trust to be revocable (you can change the terms while you are alive) or irrevocable (can't be changed; you are no longer the "owner" of the contents). A brief note here about irrevocable trusts: While they have significant and greater tax benefits, they are still subject to a Medicaid look-back

47 CNN Money. May 29, 2015. "Estate Planning: Types of Trusts." http://money.cnn.com/pf/money-essentials-trusts/. Accessed Feb. 2, 2017.

period. This means, if you transfer your assets into an irrevocable trust in an attempt to shelter them from a Medicaid spend-down, you will be ineligible for Medicaid coverage for long-term care for five years. Yet, an irrevocable trust can avoid both probate and estate taxes, and it can even protect assets from legal judgments against you.

Another thing to remember when it comes to trusts, in general, is that even if you have set up a trust, you must remember to fund it. In my 38 years' work, I've had numerous clients come to me, assuming they have protected their assets with a trust. When we talk about taxes and other pieces of their legacy, it turns out they never retitled any assets or changed any paperwork on the assets they wanted in the trust. So please remember, a trust is just fancy legal papers if you haven't followed through on retitling your assets.

Taxes

Although charitable contributions, trusts and other tax-efficient strategies can reduce your tax bill, it's unlikely that your estate will be passed on entirely tax-free. Yet, when it comes to building a legacy that can last for generations, taxes can be one of the biggest drains on the impact of your hard work.

For 2017, the federal estate exemption was $5.49 million per individual and $10.98 million for a married couple, with estates facing up to a 40 percent tax rate after that. In 2018, those limits have increased to $11.2 million for individuals and $22.4 million for married couples, with the 40 percent top level gift and estate tax remaining the same. Currently, the new estate limits are set to increase with inflation until Jan. 1, 2026, when they will "sunset" back to the inflation-adjusted 2017 limits.[48] And that's not taking into account the various state regulations and taxes regarding estate and inheritance transfers.

One "frequent flyer" on the tax concern list: retirement accounts.

Your IRA or 401(k) can be a source of tax issues when you pass away. For one thing, taking funds from a sizeable account can trigger a large tax bill. However, if you leave the assets in the account, there are still required minimum distributions (RMDs), which will take effect even after you die. If you pass the account to your spouse, he or she can keep taking your RMDs as is, or your spouse can retitle the account in his or her name and receive RMDs based on his or her life expectancy. Remember, if you don't take your RMDs, the IRS will take up to 50 percent of whatever your required distribution was, plus you will still have to pay income taxes whenever you withdraw that money. However, if you are single, divorced or widowed, or your surviving spouse will simply not need the money, you could also make a younger family member the beneficiary of your retirement account, meaning the government will recalculate RMDs based on that younger person's lifespan. This enables your beneficiary to stretch your retirement account much further than it otherwise might have gone.

Also — and this is a pretty big also — think twice before you consider putting your IRA or 401(k) in a trust. Putting an IRA in a trust means you name your trust as the owner of the IRA. But what is an IRA? It is an individual retirement account, with retirement-linked tax benefits based on the age of its owner. Let me also ask you this:

---

[48] Forbes. Dec. 21, 2018. "Final Tax Bill Includes Huge Estate Tax Win for the Rich: The $22.4 Million Exemption." https://www.forbes.com/sites/ashleaebeling/2017/12/21/final-tax-bill-includes-huge-estate-tax-win-for-the-rich-the-22-4-million-exemption/#2bf40f7d1d54. Accessed Feb. 15, 2018.

When does a "trust" reach retirement age? If your IRA is under the care of a trust, it is no longer an individual retirement account because there is no longer an individual person who owns it. Instead, it will become merely a collection of newly taxable investments. Not only will your asset then be exposed to income taxes, but the government could also exact a 10 percent tax penalty. A 10 percent penalty? You read that right. Because there is no way to calculate the approximate retirement age of a legal document (in this case, your trust), the government treats it the same as someone who has withdrawn his or her retirement funds before 59 ½. This is just one more reason to work with a financial professional, one who can strategically partner with an estate planning attorney to diligently check your decisions.

I mentioned earlier that I do meet those who feel, once they have died, "Let the living work it out," is their motto. This is, by far, a small number of people. The vast majority want an orderly distribution of their assets to those they intend to bless with the financial gifts of their lives. They want this to create as little inconvenience as possible to those who must represent the estate during the distribution process.

There is also a sizeable third group. They do not act or plan for their deaths due to various reasons, whether it is fear, procrastination or they just don't plan to ever die. To those, I would share what my grandmother taught me. She lived alone for the last 37 years of her life due to the early death of a grandfather I never knew. She had a barn about 150 yards from her house and, until my daddy was able to provide her with "running water" as we called it, she had to tote water to the barn for the farm animals. There is no telling how many gallons of water she carried to that barn. More than once, when I was helping her carry the water, she would say, "Let me help you, when you have to tote someone else's water, make it as easy as you can for them to tote it." I think that sums it up pretty well; help those who one day may be helping you.

Loss of a family member or spouse is difficult. Probate drags out that process whether you have a will or not. It can be less expensive on the estate, require less time, and reduce the probability of a mistake or family division to have a clear directive that makes your final wishes known.

CHAPTER TEN

Finding a Financial Professional

H ank and Janet sat stiffly in my conference room as I entered for our initial meeting. There was a nervousness in their voices as we greeted each other. They did not know what to expect, as they had never worked with a financial professional before, yet they were both approaching age 65 and considering retirement.

My initial meeting, which I call "Discovery," is all about learning who they are, what they want to do after work, what retirement would look like to them, and what they would see themselves doing in 10 years. Hank placed our completed questionnaire on the table before me along with their financial statements. "I'm sure you want to see these," he said. I did not reach for them. Not comfortable yet, I needed to know more about them, not just their money. I would get to their questionnaire, but before I can make recommendations about specific financial products or strategies, I have to understand their needs, listen to them talk to each other, and let them ask questions first.

For more than 40 years, they had worked, and saved. Each had contributed to a 401k, and had been saving through mutual fund companies. Janet leaned forward and said,

"I have been responsible for monitoring our investments and choosing where we would allocate our funds, and I've done a pretty good job. But I have no idea how to live off this money. I can live on a budget, but where to get the income, when do we start Social Security, how can we be more conservative so we don't get hurt by the market, and which account do we take income from first, and what money do we spend last...?...I am lost. We realize we need help."

They are like so many people I meet. They had done it themselves. They had built an estate that, along with Social Security, would be able to provide for a comfortable retirement, if they preserved their assets during the years of retirement. But there was one thing that was missing... an income plan. Or, as I call it, "The Purpose-Driven Retirement Plan." They needed to know how to take their life savings and create a plan designed to give them the income they would need to achieve a successful retirement, how to hold assets in positions that protect against loss, how to allocate assets to generate enough yield to meet future expenses, and how to hold positions for long-term growth potential to help offset inflationary pressure.

In addition to their income plan, they would have to consider estate planning, health care planning, tax planning and investment planning. You have read about how I addressed each of these areas earlier in this book. Now, let me tell you how I feel about choosing and working with an advisor. Most importantly, how you want to choose an advisor for your "station" in life.

The advisor, or "one who provides counsel," can be used in many ways, and there are various types of advisors we should consider at different stages in life. Let's explore some.

A Network of Advisors

I have shared with you about my first job right out of college and how I had to buy my first car, but let me tell you about the advisor that helped me. I was blessed with a wonderful man in my daddy. He, like many, was one of my first advisors. He, too, was blessed with a wonderful, special woman, his wife and my mother.

On the day we went car shopping, we first stopped by the bank and he introduced me to the president of the bank. I had opened a passbook savings account on my 10th birthday at that bank, and my daddy pointed that out as we discussed setting up the ability to get a loan for a new car. We next drove to the dealership where we found a car, and I watched as he negotiated with the owner of the business for the best deal he could get. Through the years, back to my grandfather, the Barnards had purchased cars from this man — more than 40 years. We then headed to the insurance agent to secure liability coverage for my new purchase and, once again, I was to meet someone with whom I would do business with for years to come. While at that shopping center, Daddy said, "There is someone else you are going to need who is a couple of doors down," so we proceeded to walk to where he introduced me to the CPA who would do my taxes for the next five years.

All in one day, over one experience, I learned a valuable lesson: Surround yourself with those who can help you navigate life. A network of go-to advisors, whatever their fields of expertise, is a valuable asset. A confidant, whom you will repeatedly need, is a must. Over the years, the role of confidant will fall into the areas of clergy, mortgage broker, insurance agent, real estate agent, accountant, health care professionals, and others. These are those people you trust, or even better, those who have been "graded" and referred to you by someone close to you. Seek experienced references for doctors, dentist, life counselors, attorneys and other advisors, just like you would a good restaurant.

Types of Financial Professionals

Locating a financial professional and deciding what type of advisor might fit your needs depends on many factors. Television, magazines and the web are filled with advertisements from financial professionals seeking your business. Others appear at your place of work periodically to fulfill the ERISA requirements of the 401(k) or 403(b) holdings. Some teach workshops or send direct mail, while others work only by being referred by current clients. Regardless of how you meet, each financial professional will hold a particular license or will have passed a qualifying exam to represent their area of expertise. Let's briefly break down the differences and some of the commonalities of various financial professionals.

Broker

A broker will typically work through a brokerage firm and represent their interest in the sale of securities. A Broker may work for an established firm, or work as an independent in the service of clients. While not an absolute, the broker will usually receive a commission from the sale of financial products or securities, but may also receive a fee for the ongoing management of those assets.

Investment Advisor Representative

An Investment Advisor Representative works through a Registered Investment Advisor and, like a broker, works with all types of securities. The investment advisor representative provides investment advice and has a fiduciary relationship, while a broker works off a suitability basis. Lastly, the investment advisor representative is typically either a fee-based or fee-only advisor — they don't receive commissions based on the sale of securities. Instead, a fee-based advisor collects fees for the management of assets, and a fee-only advisor will typically build or create a financial plan for a fee, but may not become involved in managing that individual's assets.

Insurance Producer

An insurance producer is licensed to sell insurance products, so they may work with immediate, fixed and fixed index annuities, as well as term, whole or universal life insurance policies. They work on a suitability standard, and are not licensed to provide any guidance on securities products like mutual funds, stocks, bonds, 401(k)s, etc.

Mutual Fund Companies

In addition to the different types of financial professionals, there are also options available for consumers who prefer to take matters into their own hands. Mutual fund companies promote the sale of mutual funds and exchange traded funds and the relationships with these types of organizations is primarily by phone or internet. Advisors may be available to provide information or facilitate requests, but in many cases, a licensed person must become involved to place a trade. This is usually accomplished through a "trade desk" where transactions are ordered. The mutual fund company can provide fee based service, but the general allure is low cost transaction expenses and a conduit to facilitate do-it-yourself asset management.

Self-Directed Brokerage Services

Similar to mutual fund companies, this type of brokerage service facilitates the sale and purchase of more than mutual funds. Stocks, bonds, REITS, and other stand-alone securities can be purchased and traded at reduced cost with minimal commissions or none at all. This service typically is utilized by those who do their own fund analysis, due diligence, and where trading and investing is facilitated through a trade desk.

An Accumulation Advisor

During the many years of the accumulation phase (recall my analogy of the two halves of a football game), your focus is on growing assets. You know you have a long time horizon, or period of time before you will need the dollars you have earmarked for retirement. This, depending upon your personal feelings about risk, can provide for holding the assets in growth positions. These funds will not be needed for many, many years, and can stay invested, providing growth potential. While dollars needed for income should not be exposed to risk of loss, the long-term investment can fluctuate with the tide, knowing there is a much longer time horizon for those assets to recover. As you enter the Red Zone, that period of time two to three years prior to retirement, you then begin to become conscious of market risk. A balance of investment assets that correlate with your risk feelings should always be observed in the creation of income.

There are several reasons to have access to a professional who can provide advice and direction. That information may be in the form of fee-based management or through the purchase of securities such as through a broker. Furthermore, you might engage an advisor for information to help keep you on track and make recommendations while you actually manage the assets. Any of those advisor types listed before might focus their expertise in the area of accumulation.

Do you have to have someone who manages your assets? In the accumulation phase of life, more people go without an advisor than actually use one. Millions establish a 401(k) at work and completely do it on their own. Many will look at the available options and make choices based upon the information of how the funds have performed in the past while others will read and study to create a portfolio.

I must interject here that using past performance to determine future results is no guarantee that future results will be similar. Different market conditions create different returns, which may not be replicated. If you do use this information, consider longer term averages such as the 10-year average as opposed to averages from shorter term return periods.

The Financial (Retirement) Advisor

Retirement is about income! Income that is sustainable, dependable and reliable.

Recall in the first chapter we spoke about retirement being like unemployment, but lasting for 25 to 30 years? This is where it all comes together, all your years of accumulating assets for that point in time where you will use those dollars to provide for yourself, or for two of you in the case of a couple. Those dollars must not only provide supplemental income to your Social Security and any pension, but they must also withstand illness, taxes, economic instability and, moreover, that sneaky enemy of money and time — inflation.

The runner was on second base, and George was up to bat. The team was down 5 to 4 in the last inning of the semi-finals. A fastball sped toward the plate and George drove the ball deep to center field. With two outs, the runner took off at the crack of the bat and never looked back. It was a home run. As the runner crossed the plate, George was half running and half jumping with joy, as he knew the game was won. However, in the excitement, George missed touching second base. Unaware, he continued around the diamond. A watchful eye from the other team requested that the ball be thrown back to the base and the observant umpire called the batter out — you must touch all the bases. The runner had crossed the base prior to the indiscretion, and his run would count, but the inning was over. Retirement is like this simple rule in the game of baseball. You must touch all the bases!

Structuring assets to achieve the client's income goals, plan for tax erosion, stay ahead of inflation with increasing income ability, prepare for the possibility of long-term care expenses, and then pass the remaining assets to heirs with minimum tax erosion and frustration of probate is the job of a financial advisor who specializes in helping clients prepare for retirement. All of these considerations must be built into a client's plan, as well as an investment plan that is targeted at their goals.

A Full-Service Financial Firm

I made a conscious commitment years ago to be a full-service financial firm.

As I write, we have four families who have lost loved ones and are working their way through the probate process. I have numerous clients in assisted living communities, receiving home health care or in nursing homes. I also have clients traveling and enjoying their retirements with family and friends. I see a diverse array of life experiences, circumstances and goals every day in the work I do. Being a full-service firm means, in our planning process, I am going to drill down into all aspects of the possible financial needs of the client. As I visit with a new person or couple, I am going to check-off a list that is much like the chapters of this book, with a personal relationship that can be built through trust. Important points I cover are:

Estate Plan

Are your assets positioned so, upon your (or your spouse's) death, they pass in an orderly fashion to whom you intend, free from invasive expenses or unnecessary taxes? Are both you and your spouse set so there is a proper protocol to transfer property for the first to die and second to die?

Health Care Plan

Have you protected your retirement assets from an accelerated spenddown due to both health care expenses and, more importantly, long-term care expenses? Can you self-insure due to sufficient assets, or should a plan be considered to preserve the asset base? This is especially important for couples, as the financial needs for care of the first to die can damage the ability of the asset base to provide living expenses for the surviving spouse who may also eventually have long-term care expenses.

Tax Plan

What will the effect of RMDs (forced income you cannot avoid) be on your retirement income? Will this income coupled with capital gains and earned interest on non-retirement accounts create an elevated marginal tax rate? With proper planning, many can control their eventual tax situation with early planning, while those who wait until age 70 ½ may not be as fortunate.

Income Plan

Can the asset base provide income to accommodate your wants, or will it support just your needs and preserve the income base relative to inflation and taxes until the second of the two passes? Which assets should be spent first? What is the minimum return needed to make the income plan successful and pass a legacy to heirs? The essential part of the retirement plan is the income plan, yet it is the most lacking form of planning in most homes.

Investment Plan

How will your assets be structured to accomplish all of the planning steps observed? How much risk can the assets be subjected to? The investment plan is the last part of the process for the retirement planner, in contrast to being the first part for the accumulation planner. While the accumulation of the retirement nest egg will, for the most part, focus on growth, the investment plan to provide for income in retirement will need to focus more on yield, creating real money, not just possible dollars realized only through the sale of appreciated market positions.

Whether your stage in life presents you with choosing an advisor for the accumulation phase or the distribution phase of life, make your choices based upon that particular phase. I have tried to make clear the difference in growing your money and creating a living from your money.

While in accumulation, the goal is to accumulate depending upon your level of risk acceptance for an eventual need.

During retirement, many will be faced with financing their lifestyle over an unknown number of years from a fixed amount of money, while facing the challenges of a changing landscape where they have little control. You will be faced with coordinating benefits like Social Security or a pension while determining how to draw income from taxable or tax-deferred assets in an order than minimizes taxes. You may need to plan for a surviving spouse's income in light of out-of-pocket medical expenses, paid either for the first to die or for the second to die — or both. Your retirement lifestyle will be dependent on the sustainability of your income in light of all these other factors, and that may not be something you want to be planning for all by yourself.

As a very wise man once said; seek counsel.

JEFFREY A. BARNARD

About the Author

Jeff began his career in the financial arena while still in college. While pursuing a business degree in insurance company management at the University of Alabama, he acquired his insurance license. Today, he still holds that license along with having passed the Series 65 securities examination, enabling him to act as an Investment Advisor Representative.

He regularly teaches financial workshops and seminars at churches, social clubs and community centers. Jeff enjoys the challenge of needs-based planning and he realizes that what works for one individual may not necessarily be right for another. His goal is to help clients determine where they are now and assist them in developing a strategic plan to manage assets in a way that aims to accomplish their goals.

Jeff works with clients in more than 35 different assisted living and independent living communities throughout the Atlanta Metro area. He provides investment advice, manages assets, creates financial plans for those who are transitioning from living independently in their homes to community care, and teaches workshops about financial and life care options.

Jeff is the President and CEO of Barnard Financial Group, which he has developed over more than 35 years. Barnard Financial Group is a member of an extensive network of care providers throughout the Southeast that includes estate planning attorneys, life insurance producers, professional care givers, counselors, tax professionals, home health care providers and geriatric care managers. Jeff is proud to make referrals to the professionals in this network, free of charge.

Acknowledgments

As I scan my thoughts, there are so many to whom I owe much for their support, patience and acceptance. An undertaking such as this cannot happen without the help of those who gave of their time and talents to make a dream of mine come true. Few can say they stand alone on any hill of achievement.

Having worked in the financial arena for more than 39 years, I have become the sum of countless conversations and experiences. Many people have contributed to my knowledge base; there aren't enough pages in this book to dedicate space to the gifts I have received from those who have freely given to me.

I would be remiss if I didn't begin with the love of my life, my wife, Jennifer. She remains the girl who inspires me daily. Countless hours of editing and re-reading my scribble made this book possible. Without her grace, our 35-plus years of marriage would not have been possible. I thank you, Jenny, for letting me be the one who lives your dreams.

To a mother and father who gave me a wonderful life, I wish you both could enjoy this milestone. I know you both would be proud.

Also, I have been fortunate to share the lives of my three children who have kept me chasing little feet and big plans.

Aaron, Ian and Will, I am blessed to have such wonderful young men to call my sons.

My association with Advisors Excel has changed my life's path. I thank the founders, Cody, Derek and David, for their vision and sacrifice to make their dreams come true, of which I am a benefactor. Advisors Excel has provided access to so much content that I have been able to rely and depend upon, including the training and information-sharing that made this book possible. To Stan Schroeder, who pursued me for years and did not give up, I say, again, thank you! To Victoria, Spenser and Melissa who provide support on a daily basis. I cannot do it without you, and I appreciate you, much. To the other employees of Advisors Excel, I offer my sincere gratitude to the countless service reps, new business teams, production staff, our professional receptionists and so many others who work behind the scenes to provide the support necessary to help make the dreams of so many of our clients come true. A debt of thanks to Regina Stephenson, as she has been the rock of logistics for this book. From the beginning, I knew you had my best interest at heart, and, Regina, I too did a "happy dance," only for me, it was when it was finished.

I would, of course, be lost without the support of my office staff, who service my clients and keep me moving forward, my gratitude to both Susan and Katherine.

To my clients, who for more than 39 years have given me their trust and accepted my word, I am incredibly thankful.

Above all, I owe gratitude to my Lord, Jesus Christ; through Him, all things are possible. All that I have is because of Him.